MY GIDDY AUNT

MY GIDDY AUNT

by Ray Cooney and John Chapman

CHAPPELL PLAYS

LONDON

A member of the Chappell and Intersong Music Group

First published 1970
Revised edition published 1987 by '
Chappell Plays Ltd,
(pka English Theatre Guild Ltd)
129 Park Street, London W1Y 3FA.

ISBN 0 90035 471 2

Typeset and printed by Commercial Colour Press, London E7.
Cover design by Robin Lowry.

CHARACTERS

Houseboy
Rahmu
Basil Landau
Jeremy Eppingham
Martin Eppingham
Lady Hester Eppingham
Miss Vana Lupitya
Beatrice Horrocks

N.B. The parts of Hester and Beatrice should be played by the
same actress if possible.

Act I

Scene 1	The drawing-room and verandah of Lady Eppingham's house in Janakpur, India. Late afternoon.
Scene 2	The same, next morning.

Act II

Scene 1	The same, a few minutes later.
Scene 2	The same, a moment later.
Scene 3	The same, that night.
Time	The present

Application for permission to perform this play
in the United Kingdom should be made to:-

WARNER/CHAPPELL PLAYS LTD
(formerly English Theatre Guild Ltd)

Griffin House, 161 Hammersmith Road
London W6 8BS
Tel 0181 563 5888 Fax 0181 563 5801

J.4

NOTE

The photographs included in this edition were taken by Kenneth Broome from the Opera House Theatre Jersey production of *My Giddy Aunt*.

MY GIDDY AUNT was first produced at the Grand Theatre, Wolverhampton on 25 September 1967 with the following cast:

RAHMU	Garry Taylor
BASIL LANDAU	John Shorter
JEREMY EPPINGHAM	Gerald Moon
MARTIN EPPINGHAM	Kevin Smith
LADY HESTER	Carole Allen
MISS VANA LUPITYA	Mary Mitchell
BEATRICE HORROCKS	Carole Allen

Directed by Ronnie Scott-Dodd

The play was subsequently produced by Ray Cooney Productions in association with Le Clare Productions at the Savoy Theatre, London, on 20 June 1968, with the following cast:

HOUSEBOY	Roger Carey
RAHMU	Manning Wilson
BASIL LANDAU	Peter Gray
JEREMY EPPINGHAM	Guy Slater
MARTIN EPPINGHAM	Charles Stapley
LADY HESTER	Irene Handl
MISS VANA LUPITYA	Margo Johns
BEATRICE HORROCKS	Irene Handl

Directed by Wallace Douglas

The play was revised and produced by Dick Ray at the Opera House Theatre, Jersey on 15 July 1986, with the following cast:

HOUSEBOY	Daniel Blair
RAHMU	Michael Lomax
BASIL LANDAU	William Moore
JEREMY EPPINGHAM	Paul Laidlaw
MARTIN EPPINGHAM	Peter Denyer
LADY HESTER	Mollie Sugden
MISS VANA LUPITYA	Janet Edis
BEATRICE HORROCKS	Mollie Sugden

Directed by Jimmy Thompson

photograph by Kenneth Broome from the Jersey Opera House Theatre production.

ACT ONE
Scene One

The set is the drawing-room and verandah of LADY HESTER
EPPINGHAM'S *house at the foothills of the Himalayas. The drawing-
room takes up most of the stage but three steps go up to an arch with
beaded curtains L. leading to a small verandah. The verandah has steps
leading down from it into the shrubbery L. In the U.R. corner of the
drawing-room, at an angle, are the double doors leading into the main
hallway. D.L. of the drawing-room is a curtained see-through door
leading onto a narrow balcony which is the continuation of the verandah.*

*Although the action takes place in the present day the general decor is very
Colonial India. There is an atmosphere of decay about the place. The
walls are decorated with animals' heads, old paintings, Army photographs
and a portrait of George V and Mary. Against the wall R. is an ornate
glass-fronted gun cabinet. D.R. of this is a flat-top desk. There is a
round table D.R.C around which are three chairs; also another chair by
the desk. The settee is D.L.C. with a small stool D.L. In front of the
verandah (but leaving room to pass above the settee) is a drinks cupboard
on which stands glasses, whisky etc. and an old-fashioned telephone.
U.C. to the left of the main doors is an old-fashioned gramophone.*

*It is 6 p.m. when the curtain rises and there are background noises of
birds. The drawing-room section is in semi-darkness because the blinds
are drawn across the French windows with the afternoon sun filtering
through. At the moment the stage is empty but after a couple of seconds the
double doors are opened by the* HOUSEBOY. *He is followed in by*
RAHMU, LADY HESTER'S *Indian Servant.* RAHMU *is aged about 50,
nimble and anxious to please. Last to enter is* BASIL LANDAU, *a solicitor
carrying a briefcase. He is precise and slightly pompous.* LANDAU *enters
to L. of door, hands hat to* RAHMU. *He hands it to the* HOUSEBOY.

RAHMU	Will you wait in here please, Sahib?
LANDAU	(*crosses L. above sofa*) Yes. I — er — take it I am expected?
RAHMU	Yes Sahib, would you care to sit down?
	(RAHMU *and* HOUSEBOY *start to exit.*)
LANDAU	(*seeing rhinoceros head on the wall*) Good God!
RAHMU	Did you speak, Sahib?
LANDAU	No. (*Takes papers out of briefcase, and places on table.*)

RAHMU	I do not think her Ladyship will keep you waiting too long.
LANDAU	I hope not. I'm catching the train back to Bombay this evening.
RAHMU	I will inform her of your wish. (*He bows.*)
LANDAU	It's not so much my wish as my intention.
RAHMU	You must remember, Sahib, Lady Eppingham is getting on in years.

(*He bows and exits U.C.* LANDAU *follows, surveys, returns to table. Places briefcase under table, when seated. Puts on glasses. Looks through papers.* JEREMY *enters stealthily onto verandah, crosses to L. of* LANDAU. JEREMY *is in his early 20s, & is not as normal as he appears.*)

JEREMY	I say —
LANDAU	(*rising startled*) Good God. (*Takes off glasses.*)
JEREMY	Sorry.
LANDAU	I didn't hear you come in.
JEREMY	That was the idea.
LANDAU	Oh. (*Sits.*)
JEREMY	Anyone looking after you?
LANDAU	Er — yes, thank you. Your man is informing her Ladyship of my arrival.
JEREMY	You'll be lucky. She'll be fast asleep. Like a drink?
LANDAU	Little early isn't it?
JEREMY	Please yourself. (*Takes bottle out.*) You don't mind if I do — ?
LANDAU	No.

(JEREMY *pours large drink, adds the smallest splash of soda, then to above sofa again.*)

JEREMY	Are you sure you won't join me?
LANDAU	Well, perhaps I will. But only a double please.

(JEREMY *chuckles and goes back to drinks, puts glass down, pours drink for* LANDAU.)

JEREMY   Soda?

LANDAU   Please.

(JEREMY *adds soda, then crosses to* LANDAU *with drinks.*)

JEREMY   (*handing drink*) Your very good health.

LANDAU   And yours. (*He drinks.*)

JEREMY   What a shame there's no one here to introduce us.

LANDAU   That shouldn't prove an insuperable problem. My name's Landau.

JEREMY   Ah.

LANDAU   Basil Landau.

JEREMY   Ah, that's nice. (*Sits.*) Nobody told me to expect a Basil Landau.

LANDAU   Possibly not. We wrote to Lady Eppingham.

JEREMY   That was a pointless thing to do. She won't have read it.

LANDAU   Your servant said she was expecting me.

JEREMY   Oh. (*Rising.*) You've never met her have you?

LANDAU   No.

JEREMY   (*laughing, crosses to gramophone, U.L.*) Ah, well, never mind. (*He puts on a record of weird Indian music.*) You're not by any chance from the police, are you?

LANDAU   Good heavens no. Are you expecting them?

JEREMY   (*grinning*) Not yet. You must be in the tea planting business.

LANDAU   I'm a solicitor.

JEREMY   Oh, in everybody's business.

LANDAU	We have our uses.
JEREMY	Yes. (*Crosses to sofa and sits.*)
LANDAU	(*getting annoyed at* JEREMY'S *manner*) I asked your servant to tell Lady Eppingham that my time was limited.
JEREMY	Not as limited as hers. (*Drinks.*)
	(MARTIN *enters. He is in his mid-30s, very masculine and the full charmer.*)
MARTIN	My dear fellow. I'm frightfully sorry. (LANDAU *rises.*) Martin. (*Shakes hands.*)
LANDAU	Mm?
MARTIN	Lady Eppingham's nephew.
LANDAU	Oh, how do you do.
MARTIN	I would have been here to meet you, but one has to put in the odd appearance round the estate. Keep some sort of eye on the natives. You've met my brother, haven't you?
LANDAU	(*turning to face* JEREMY) Your — ? Oh, yes. He very kindly gave me a drink.
MARTIN	Splendid. Just the job. Do sit down. (*He does.*) Glad he's been entertaining you. Good boy, Jeremy.
JEREMY	(*rising*) You didn't tell me about that letter.
MARTIN	Mm?
JEREMY	From the solicitor.
MARTIN	That wasn't for you. That was for Aunt Hester. (*To* LANDAU.) I cope with her affairs. So, what's it all about?
LANDAU	I would prefer to discuss it with Lady Eppingham.
MARTIN	Hasn't Jeremy told you about her?
LANDAU	No.

MARTIN	(*after a short pause*) It's her age I suppose. She gets a bit muddled.
LANDAU	Muddled?
MARTIN	Legal documents tend to confuse her. (*To* JEREMY *irritably.*) Stop playing that damn piano, will you?!
JEREMY	Temper. (*Crosses to gramophone.*)
LANDAU	Then my business here looks as though it may be somewhat protracted.
MARTIN	Quite.
	(JEREMY *takes off record.*)
LANDAU	Possibly I could discuss the matter with her husband then?
MARTIN	I'm afraid Aunt Hester is a widow. Sir Harry died years ago.
LANDAU	Oh!
MARTIN	So I suggest you tell me what you've come about.
LANDAU	(*weakening*) In view of what I have to disclose, Lady Eppingham really ought to be present.
MARTIN	(*to desk, to get papers from drawer*) It's curious, you know, but in the past, all my Aunt's affairs have been conducted by a firm of solicitors in London. (JEREMY *sits on arm of sofa.*) Cooper, Cooper and Hill.
LANDAU	Yes, that is so.
MARTIN	Ah, you're a member of that firm are you?
LANDAU	No. Cooper, Cooper and Hill have instructed us to conduct this matter on their behalf. The personal touch, you understand. However, if you say that legal documents might confuse Lady Eppingham —
JEREMY	Definitely!

LANDAU	And as Sir Harry is deceased, I think perhaps I will give you the salient details.
MARTIN	It'll save time I assure you. (*Rising to L. of* LANDAU.) My aunt leaves a good deal of the paper work to me. She's quite happy to potter about the place supervising the gardens while I run the tea business.
JEREMY	(*sitting up*) With my help. You tell us what it's all about, Mr Landau.
LANDAU	Yes. Well, briefly it concerns your aunt's father.
MARTIN	(*alert*) Lord Rothbury?
LANDAU	Yes. I regret he died last week.
JEREMY	(*rising*) Great!
	(LANDAU *turns, surprised.*)
MARTIN	Jeremy!
JEREMY	What took him so long? He was about a hundred.
LANDAU	Ninety-eight, to be precise.
JEREMY	(*crouching*) Well, be a little more precise, and tell us how he split the proceeds.
MARTIN	(*stepping in*) You must excuse my brother, but for years the old boy has kept Aunt Hester on a shoestring.
LANDAU	I gather he very kindly allowed her to live here, and yourselves?
JEREMY	Big deal!
MARTIN	We've done all the work, and he's just sat back in England collecting all the profits.
LANDAU	Presumably you've received a salary? Made a living?
JEREMY	You call this living? Nothing has been altered here since Sir Harry died.
LANDAU	Well, if you'll forgive my asking, why have you put up with it?

MARTIN	(*leaning on table*) We've been waiting, Mr Landau.
LANDAU	Waiting?
MARTIN	For today. (*He sits down.*)
LANDAU	Oh.
JEREMY	Proceed.
LANDAU	(*putting on glasses*) Yes. Well, the Will is quite straightforward.
JEREMY	Good.
LANDAU	This tea estate is left to his sole surviving relative, Lady Eppingham. (*Puts glasses on table.*)
JEREMY	That was the least he could do.
MARTIN	Well, what else?
LANDAU	Nothing.
MARTIN	Nothing? But he must have been worth a fortune. Who the hell gets that?
LANDAU	His estate in Norfolk he bequeathed to the National Trust.
MARTIN	(*rising*) What?
LANDAU	Presumably to cut down on the death duties which still amounted to £250,000.
MARTIN	(*to desk*) Good God.
JEREMY	(*stepping in*) You mean the British Government picks up a quarter of a million, the National Trust gets half Norfolk and Auntie gets nothing but this place?
LANDAU	The annual income from this estate is quite considerable. In 1960, (*Refers to papers.*), it amounted to £20,000.
JEREMY	(*looking at* MARTIN) Yes, well it's nothing like that now, I can tell you.
LANDAU	Mm? (*Turns over pages.*) No, you're right. It's halved in the last ten years.

MARTIN	That's because Lord Rothbury wouldn't plough back any of his damn profits into modernising the place.
JEREMY	Quite, quite. (*Eyeing* MARTIN.)
LANDAU	Even so, it's a considerable drop in such a short period.
	(*There is a knock and* RAHMU *enters, followed by the* HOUSEBOY.)
RAHMU	Sahib.
MARTIN	What is it?
RAHMU	Memsahib says she won't keep you a moment.
MARTIN	Tell her I've dealt with it.
LANDAU	Yes, don't disturb her on my account.
AUNTIE	(*entering*) Tell the Viceroy to tether his elephant while I sober up my husband.
	(AUNTIE *sweeps through double doors. She is seventy years of age, wearing a full length 1930 style green lace evening gown and cloak. She carries a fan. Her grey hair is topped by a tiara. For many years she has been somewhat eccentric and decidedly vague. However, she's very sprightly and full of fun.*)
	(*to* LANDAU) Ah, there you are, Harry. Don't drink too much before the Ball, darling. (*She takes the glass from the astonished* LANDAU *and gives it to* RAHMU.) Why don't you keep an eye on my husband?
RAHMU	Yes, Memsahib.
AUNTIE	(*to* LANDAU) You're not even dressed yet, Harry.
LANDAU	(*nervously*) I'm Landau, Lady Eppingham. Basil Landau. (*He proffers his hand.*)
AUNTIE	(*slapping hand*) Oh, don't be silly. There'll be ample opportunity to dance at the ball.

LANDAU	I beg your pardon?
AUNTIE	You should see me dance the polka, la, la.
MARTIN	(*to* AUNTIE, *C.*) Come and sit down, Aunt. (*He leads her to chair.*)
AUNTIE	Don't bully me, Martin, or you won't get any pocket money. (*Sits.*) Jeremy, get Auntie a drink.
MARTIN	You know what the doctor said.
AUNTIE	Fiddlesticks. Get me a large brandy.
	(JEREMY *goes to drinks.*)
LANDAU	(*stepping in*) Lady Eppingham —
AUNTIE	(*turns to him*) Ah, come in doctor.
	(LANDAU *looks about him.*)
MARTIN	We tried to explain that you wouldn't wish to see him.
AUNTIE	Quite right. Hate doctors. Always have.
LANDAU	I'm not a doctor.
AUNTIE	Doesn't seem to stop you from practising.
LANDAU	I'm a solicitor.
AUNTIE	Yes, of course you are. I've been waiting for you, haven't I.
LANDAU	Have you? Oh, that's a relief. (*Smiles at brothers.*)
AUNTIE	I think I should get away with manslaughter, don't you?
	(LANDAU *looks at her. His smile fades.*)
MARTIN	(*warningly*) Aunt Hester.
AUNTIE	(*to* LANDAU) Well, nobody deserved it more than Harry.
LANDAU	Your husband?
AUNTIE	I caught him philandering with that native girl. Had to shoot him didn't I?

Lady Hester Eppingham

Lady Hester and Landau

LANDAU	Shoot? Oh (*laughs to humour her*) — yes, yes, of course.
RAHMU	(*to R. of* AUNTIE) Please Memsahib, do not distress yourself. This solicitor is Mr Basil Landau.
AUNTIE	Ah, well, he's bound to spout at some length. Better tell the Viceroy to go on without us.
RAHMU	Yes Memsahib. (*Exits with* LANDAU's *glass.*)
AUNTIE	(*facing* LANDAU) So you're a solicitor are you? Are you Copper, Cooper, or Hill?
LANDAU	I'm from Bombay.
AUNTIE	You see, they never give you a straight answer, these lawyers.
MARTIN	Mr Landau is with a firm in Bombay.
	(JEREMY *starts to cross with drink.*)
AUNTIE	Is he?
JEREMY	Here's your poison, Auntie.
AUNTIE	Thank you, dear boy. I shall miss these two when they go back to school. Cheers everybody. (*To* LANDAU.) And a long life to you, Harry my darling. (*Drinks.*)
LANDAU	Er — cheers.
AUNTIE	Now, what were you saying, Mr Landau?
MARTIN	He's called to see you on important business, Aunt.
AUNTIE	Yes, Cooper, Cooper and Hill.
MARTIN	Mr Landau has nothing to do with them.
AUNTIE	Don't blame him. They're a lot of scoundrels.
LANDAU	Lady Eppingham, if I could just briefly reiterate —
AUNTIE	Yes, do by all means. Jeremy, show this gentleman where.

	(LANDAU *reacts to this.*)
JEREMY	(*crosses to drinks*) Yes Auntie. Er — can I top you up?
LANDAU	I think not.
AUNTIE	(*to* LANDAU) Get on with it, darling. The Viceroy is waiting for us.
LANDAU	Lady Eppingham, if I could have your undivided attention —
	(JEREMY *laughs.*)
AUNTIE	Did I say something funny, Jeremy?
JEREMY	(*turning at drinks*) No, Auntie. Mr Landau did.
AUNTIE	Mr Landau? Who's that?
LANDAU	I am Mr Landau.
AUNTIE	Don't keep introducing yourself, it's very irritating.
LANDAU	The London firm of Cooper, Cooper and Hill have instructed me to call on you personally, owing to the distressing nature of their news.
AUNTIE	How very thoughtful. Has something happened to the tea shares?
LANDAU	No, no, no.
AUNTIE	They've been going down steadily for years, you know.
LANDAU	Yes, so I gather, but that's not what I came about.
AUNTIE	Oh, well it was very nice of you to call, especially with all this show. Goodbye.
	(LANDAU *looks bewildered.* MARTIN *takes* AUNTIE's *arm.*)
MARTIN	There's something else, Aunt.
LANDAU	Yes, I'm afraid it concerns your father.

AUNTIE	My father? Good Lord, that fellow's not still alive, is he?
LANDAU	Last week, Lord Rothbury, aged ninety-eight, met an untimely end.
AUNTIE	(*laughing*) Hardly untimely at ninety-eight.
LANDAU	(*levelling off*) Would you care to know the details, Lady Eppingham?
AUNTIE	I think this dress has faded in the sun.
LANDAU	(*confused at this sudden change of thought*) I beg your pardon?
AUNTIE	(*referring to dress*) Would you say this was pink?
LANDAU	(*helpfully*) Er — yes, I suppose so.
AUNTIE	Yes. Well there you are then. It used to be green. (*Sits on sofa.*) I'll have some more brandy, Jeremy.
JEREMY	Don't you want to know about Lord Rothbury, Auntie?
AUNTIE	I know all about him, you fool. He's my father. Middle-aged roué. (*To* LANDAU.) Always very civil to me though. Probably because I'm the only one, apple of his eye and all that. Took me to my coming-out ball last week. That's where I met Harry. Do you know the impetuous lad wants me to marry him, and go out to India? I'm much too young, of course. But, as my father has a tea estate out there, I might just do it.
	(MARTIN *rises, foot on desk chair.* JEREMY *rises, with glass, goes to drinks cupboard.*)
JEREMY	I'll get you a brandy, Auntie.
LANDAU	(*edging U.S. hands glass to* JEREMY) And I'll change my mind, if I may.
JEREMY	Join the club.

AUNTIE	Go on, Mr Landau, go on.
LANDAU	(*steps to* AUNTIE) Mm? I beg your pardon?
AUNTIE	You were saying about Lord Rothbury.
LANDAU	Was I? Oh, yes.
AUNTIE	Well, what about him?
LANDAU	Died.
AUNTIE	(*holds dress*) No, just faded.
	(LANDAU *closes his eyes in anguish.*)
MARTIN	By the way, how did it happen?
AUNTIE	I've told you, the sun.
	(MARTIN *sits on chair.* JEREMY *crosses to above R. end of sofa.*)
LANDAU	I'm sure Lady Eppingham will be happy to know that her father died in harness.
AUNTIE	How on earth did he come to do that?
LANDAU	During a debate in the House of Lords, he was found to be dead.
AUNTIE	How could they tell?
JEREMY	Here's your brandy, Auntie.
AUNTIE	Thank you.
JEREMY	(*handing drink to* LANDAU) Mr Landau.
LANDAU	It was his heart.
AUNTIE	(*drinks*) Yes, it would be.
LANDAU	The point is, as I've already explained to your nephews —
AUNTIE	No they're not my nephews. They're Harry's brother's boys. (*Rising.*) Didn't have any children of our own, so only too pleased to give them a home. What are you doing with my wool? Do you know Harry's brother?
LANDAU	No.

AUNTIE	You don't know much, do you. (*Cross to L. of table.*) Ring that bell will you, Doctor.
LANDAU	(*cross to table. Rings hand-bell*) Er — yes.
AUNTIE	I want to ask Rahmu if he's watered the Viceroy's elephant.
LANDAU	I was saying that under the terms of the Will, you are to inherit this tea estate.
AUNTIE	Oh, Harry will be pleased.
LANDAU	Yes, I'm sure he will. The estate in Norfolk your father bequeathed to the National Trust.
MARTIN	(*crosses to desk*) Everything else had to be sold to pay death duties.
AUNTIE	Death duties? Somebody died?
LANDAU	Your father, Lord Rothbury.
AUNTIE	(*looking around*) Where?
MARTIN	He's died.
JEREMY	Mr Landau has very kindly come all this way from Bombay to tell us that you've inherited this estate and Martin and I have got Sweet Fanny Adams.
AUNTIE	Really? (*To* LANDAU.) Ring that thing again will you?
	(LANDAU *crosses to above table and rings bell.*)
	How much exactly went into death duties, Mr Landau?
LANDAU	Something in the region of a quarter of a million pounds.
AUNTIE	Good gracious. That's iniquitous.
JEREMY	(*rising to L. of* AUNTIE) Don't upset yourself Auntie. At least you've got this estate. Martin and I have got nothing.
AUNTIE	(*patting his face*) What about that sweet Adams girl?

(*There is a knock at the door.*)

Let her in will you. (JEREMY *crosses to above sofa.*)

MARTIN	Come in.

(RAHMU *enters.*)

RAHMU	You rang, Memsahib?
AUNTIE	I don't think so. Did I?
MARTIN	No, clear off.
RAHMU	I thought I am hearing bells.
MARTIN	Get out.
AUNTIE	Martin, don't be such a bully. If Rahmu hears bells, you should treat him gently. Now, tell us all about it, Rahmu.
LANDAU	(*steps to R. of* AUNTIE) I rang the bell, Lady Eppingham.
AUNTIE	Whatever for?
LANDAU	(*awkwardly*) Something to do with the elephant.
AUNTIE	Elephant? What elephant?
LANDAU	(*looks from* MARTIN *to* JEREMY, *doubtfully*) The Viceroy's?
AUNTIE	My dear Mr Landau, you're wandering. There hasn't been a Viceroy in India for years.
MARTIN	All right, Rahmu, all right. (*Sits on desk.*)
RAHMU	Very good Sahib. (*He bows, and starts to exit.* LANDAU *stops him.*)
LANDAU	Be good enough to tell the driver of my taxi I won't be very long now.
AUNTIE	Taxi?
LANDAU	It's outside.
AUNTIE	We don't want a taxi, Harry. We're going to the Ball on the Viceroy's elephant. That's all, Rahmu.

RAHMU	Very good, Memsahib. (*Exits.*)
LANDAU	Lady Eppingham, I have to be at the station.
AUNTIE	When you start to get formal, Harry, I know you're cross with me.
MARTIN	Have you anything else to tell us, Mr Landau?
LANDAU	(*hurriedly collecting papers, and putting in briefcase*) I don't think so. Cooper, Cooper and Hill will be forwarding a photostat copy of the Will, and when we've had a perusal of it, we'll send it on to you.
AUNTIE	I shouldn't bother, I shall contest.
LANDAU	(*facing her*) Contest?
AUNTIE	Most certainly. How should one go about that, Mr Landau?
LANDAU	Well — er, basically there are only two grounds for taking such a course of action.
AUNTIE	Well, come on then. Let's have them.
LANDAU	Firstly, if it could be shown that at the time the Will was drawn up, Lord Rothbury was Non Compos Mentis —
AUNTIE	Oh, he was always that.
LANDAU	There was absolutely nothing to show that your father was anything but normal.
AUNTIE	What about wearing a harness in the House of Lords?
JEREMY	Mr Landau, what's the second requirement for contesting?
LANDAU	If you suffered financial hardship by being badly treated in the Will.
AUNTIE	That's the one. We'll go for that.
LANDAU	I'm afraid your case would be very slim.
AUNTIE	Why?

LANDAU	You've inherited this estate.
AUNTIE	My good man, it's very difficult to live off this. The crop is appalling. We must be the only tea growers in India who have to drink instant coffee.
LANDAU	It isn't only the annual income which would affect the issue.
JEREMY	Well, there's nothing else is there.
LANDAU	Most certainly. The Attorney General would have to take into consideration the capital value of the place.
AUNTIE	I've just told you. There is no value.
LANDAU	If you choose to sell, I'm sure it would realise at least 100,000.
MARTIN	(*suddenly interested*) Pounds?
LANDAU	(*facing* MARTIN) Yes.
MARTIN	That sounds interesting.
AUNTIE	Sell it? Never. The Rothburys have been in India for 200 years.
LANDAU	But if you were pleading poverty to the Attorney General —
AUNTIE	You can tell the Attorney General that he will evict me only over my dead body. Who the hell does he think he is?
LANDAU	Lady Eppingham, we're dealing with a hypothesis.
AUNTIE	Yes, and a very dangerous one. You can tell him that if he puts one foot in Janakpur, or attempts to molest me in any way, I shall arm the natives. (*To* JEREMY.) What was I saying?
JEREMY	You were explaining our precarious financial situation, Auntie.
AUNTIE	Ah, yes. Martin, what was the turnover for last year?

MARTIN	I don't know.
AUNTIE	Of course you do. You keep the books.
MARTIN	Yes.
AUNTIE	We'd be a lot better off if you concentrated on your work out here, instead of philandering with your lady friends.

(JEREMY *laughs, and goes to drinks cupboard.*)

AUNTIE	(*To* JEREMY) And if you could keep your face out of a whisky glass for five minutes together, you might be of some help. (*To* LANDAU.) Spongers, both of them. Women and drink. Take after Sir Harry of course, only he did both at once. (*Laughing cheerfully.*) One rather admired him for it.

(JEREMY *crosses to drinks and pours one.*)

MARTIN	Considering the pittance we get, this place is run damn well.
AUNTIE	Rubbish.
JEREMY	Mr Landau, do you advise us to contest or not?
LANDAU	Well, that's really up to Lady Eppingham.
AUNTIE	Oh, I'm up to it all right.
MARTIN	(*rising then crosses to door*) Well, fortunately we don't have to decide on it tonight. What about your train, Landau?
JEREMY	We could decide tonight.
MARTIN	(*with quiet menace*) I said leave it.
LANDAU	Yes, well I really must be going. Here's my card, Lady Eppingham.
AUNTIE	(*rising and taking card*) I'll mark the last waltz down for you.
LANDAU	I'm leaving now.
AUNTIE	Leaving?

LANDAU	Yes. I must.
MARTIN	(*stepping in*) I'll see you out. Cheerio, Landau.
AUNTIE	I won't have it. It's only a twenty minute ride to the station, and you've got your elephant, haven't you?
MARTIN	Mr Landau has to go, Aunt.
AUNTIE	Very well then. You see him out. (*Taking* LANDAU's *arm.*) Harry and I are just going to water the lawn.
LANDAU	(*miserably going with her*) This really must be brief, Lady Eppingham.
AUNTIE	Yes, yes, yes, Harry. Would you believe it, snowing again.
	(*They exit to verandah.*)
MARTIN	Crazy old fool. £100,000, eh.
JEREMY	Looks like we'll just have to wait until she kicks the bucket.
MARTIN	(*smiling*) Yes.
JEREMY	Lucky for us Carradine's on his way, isn't it?
MARTIN	(*turning on him*) What do you know about Carradine?
JEREMY	(*crosses to drinks*) Only that you phoned just now to see if he'd left. Why've you asked him again? Last time he wouldn't put her away.
MARTIN	Last time I couldn't afford it.
JEREMY	Has he dropped his price?
MARTIN	No.
JEREMY	I see, so that's why you've stepped up your fiddling.

MARTIN	What d'you mean?
JEREMY	Oh, I don't mind. So long as you keep the cellar well stocked. But you want to be careful you know. Auntie might change her Will if she knew you were selling half the tea on the side.
MARTIN	Where the hell did you get that information from?
JEREMY	Little brother's watching you.
MARTIN	Yes. And I don't like it.
JEREMY	(*turns viciously*) And I don't like being kept in the dark so much. (*Quietly smiling.*) We were going to do this together. (*Sits on sofa.*) I might have to start making my own arrangements.
MARTIN	What are you talking about?
JEREMY	For Auntie's departure. You spend too much time and money on your women. I suppose you've still got that expensive girl in Janakpur.
MARTIN	No.
JEREMY	Oh, found out about the one in Calcutta, did she?
RAHMU	(*entering*) Excuse me, Sahib.
MARTIN	What is it?
RAHMU	Two ladies have arrived.
MARTIN	Two ladies?
JEREMY	(*to* MARTIN) Got a double booking. (*Laughs.*)
RAHMU	They are hoping to find Landau Sahib here.
MARTIN	Landau? You'd better ask them to come in, I suppose.
RAHMU	Very good, Sahib.

(RAHMU *bows then goes to the door, opens it and reveals the* HOUSEBOY. RAHMU *gives him instructions and he ushers in* MISS VANA LUPITYA. *She is a beautiful, young Indian woman. She is very businesslike and carries a briefcase.* RAHMU *tells the* HOUSEBOY *to go. He exits with* VANA'S *suitcase.*)

VANA   Good evening. I hope I am in time to catch Mr Landau.

JEREMY   (*having risen*) Only just, I'm afraid. He was about to set off on his safari back to Bombay. Rahmu, rescue him from her Ladyship will you? They're on the lawn somewhere.

RAHMU   Yes, Sahib. (*He exits through verandah.*)

VANA   I must apologise for my unheralded visit.

MARTIN   Don't apologise. I'm delighted.

VANA   I am Miss Vana Lupitya.

MARTIN   (*shaking her hand, very warmly*) How do you do. Martin Eppingham.

VANA   How do you do, Mr Eppingham.

            (JEREMY *coughs.*)

MARTIN   My brother Jeremy.

VANA   I am very pleased to make your acquaintance. (*They shake hands.*)

JEREMY   That goes for me, too. (*Grins at* MARTIN.)

VANA   I am a business colleague of Mr Landau's.

MARTIN   Not the same firm, surely?

VANA   Yes. But of course, I am only a junior partner.

JEREMY   You can't be a solicitor?

VANA   Why not?

MARTIN   Far too attractive.

VANA	Does this mean you would not avail yourself of my services?
MARTIN	On the contrary. Can I get you a drink, Miss Lupitya?
VANA	Yes, thank you.
MARTIN	Whisky, brandy, sherry . . .
VANA	A glass of sherry, please.
	(MARTIN *goes to drinks and pours a sherry.*)
JEREMY	Please, Miss Lupitya, won't you sit down?
VANA	Thank you.
	(*They sit.*)
MARTIN	Medium dry. How's that?
VANA	Yes, thank you.
MARTIN	Rahmu said something about two ladies —
VANA	Ah, yes. Mrs Horrocks.
MARTIN	Mrs Horrocks?
VANA	I asked her to wait in the taxi outside. I wanted to see Mr Landau before asking her in.
AUNTIE	(*entering*) If this is my dressmaker, Harry, I'll tell her it used to be green and it's shrunk.
	(MARTIN *crosses to L.* VANA *rises, crosses to below table with drink and briefcase.* RAHMU, AUNTIE *and* LANDAU *appear on verandah.*)
MARTIN	She's Landau's partner.
AUNTIE	(*to* VANA) I've booked him for the last waltz.
LANDAU	Miss Lupitya is with my firm, Lady Eppingham.
AUNTIE	All right, all right.
LANDAU	I was merely reiterating.
AUNTIE	Well don't. It's a very unpleasant habit of yours.

(RAHMU *holds open bead curtains, and* AUNTIE *and* LANDAU *pass through.* AUNTIE *pokes* RAHMU.)
Go on.

RAHMU   Memsahib?

AUNTIE   Announce us, you fool.

RAHMU   (*entering room*) Lady Eppingham.

AUNTIE   (*tapping* RAHMU's *shoulder*) Both of us. (*To* LANDAU.) Rahmu will never understand protocol, you know.

RAHMU   (*crosses to* AUNTIE) Who is the gentleman please?

AUNTIE   (*to* LANDAU) I am sorry about this, Harry.

RAHMU   Sir Harry and Lady Eppingham.

(AUNTIE *takes* LANDAU's *arm and enters to L. of* VANA. LANDAU *remains C.* AUNTIE *shakes* VANA's *hand.*)

AUNTIE   Ah, Lady Abercrombie, delighted to see you. You must be very careful out here, Lady Abercrombie. I see you've caught the sun a bit already.

MARTIN   (*stepping to below sofa*) Aunt Hester, let me introduce you to Miss Lupitya.

VANA   How do you do, Lady Eppingham.

AUNTIE   You should try calamine lotion. Give her a prescription, doctor.

VANA   Doctor?

LANDAU   (*over shoulder to* AUNTIE) One moment, please. (*They cross D.R.*) Miss Lupitya, what on earth brings you here.

(MARTIN *crosses to above L. of sofa.*)

VANA   Your clerk thought it imperative that I should reach you before you left.

LANDAU   Why, for heaven's sake?

VANA	(*quietly*) The unexpected arrival of Mrs Horrocks.
LANDAU	Mrs — ? Do I know the lady?
AUNTIE	You're not to whisper, doctor. If there's anything radically wrong with me, I have a right to know.
JEREMY	(*moving closer to* AUNTIE) They're discussing business, Auntie.
AUNTIE	Well, they're not going to do that in my house. Haven't you got an office, Mr Landau?
LANDAU	(*turning to face* AUNTIE) Indeed I have. Would that I were there now, instead of in this —
JEREMY	Careful now.
LANDAU	(*to* VANA) Miss Lupitya, I will be leaving here within the next few minutes to catch the 8.17 train to Bombay, by way of Patna. I suggest you accompany me and, during the journey, you can tell me whatever you have to tell me about this Mrs . . . er . . .
AUNTIE	Horrocks.
LANDAU	(*turns surprised to* AUNTIE) Hm?
AUNTIE	Horrocks.
LANDAU	Precisely.
VANA	Mr Landau, I am afraid that until this matter is cleared up, neither of us can leave.
AUNTIE	Oh, splendid. Martin, go and tell Rahmu to air the double bed in the blue room.
	(LANDAU *reacts embarrassed to* MISS LUPITYA *who smiles.*)
MARTIN	(*crosses onto verandah*) Why don't you move your whole damn firm up here and have done with it? (*Shouting.*) Rahmu.
AUNTIE	If you must shout, do it quietly, Martin. (MARTIN *drops down on verandah.*)

JEREMY	What about this Mrs Horrocks who's waiting outside?
AUNTIE	(*to* MARTIN) Oh, yes. Tell her it used to be green and what is more, it has shrunk.

(RAHMU *enters on verandah.*)

RAHMU	You called, Sahib?
AUNTIE	He shouted, Rahmu.
MARTIN	Another lady arrived with Miss Lupitya.
RAHMU	Yes, Sahib.
MARTIN	Show her in.
RAHMU	Very good, Sahib. (RAHMU *bows and exits.*)
MARTIN	Well come on then. What's it all about?
VANA	(*handing letter to* LANDAU) This letter will alter things very considerably.
MARTIN	In what way alter?
AUNTIE	It needs at least two inches on the hem.
LANDAU	Will you allow me to —
AUNTIE	Of course. You're my lawyer, you must get my story straight.

(VANA *crosses to table and puts down briefcase.*)

LANDAU	Yes, of course. What story?
AUNTIE	How I came to murder my husband. (*Rising.*) Tell them it was suicide, or a shooting accident.

(MARTIN *and* JEREMY *stiffen.*)

LANDAU	Yes, yes, of course. (*Goes onto verandah.*)
AUNTIE	(*crosses to verandah*) Come along, come along, now I'm going to give you both a cutting from my Japonika. It's an absolute picture at this time of year. (*Looking off U.L.*) Martin, the locusts have denuded my fir tree again. Oh no! It's alright. It's the flagpole. (*Exits U.L. verandah.*)

JEREMY	I know. Mrs Horrocks represents the National Trust and she's flown over to grab a piece of the estate as well.
VANA	To the best of my knowledge Mrs Horrocks is in no way connected with that organisation.
JEREMY	Bully for her.
MARTIN	Well, just what is she concerned with then?
VANA	I'll leave Mr Landau to explain both that and the Codicil.
JEREMY	Aye — aye.
MARTIN	What Codicil?
VANA	To Lord Rothbury's Will. Apparently it was lodged with his bank and was not discovered until three days after the Will had been opened.
LANDAU	(*crosses to chair and sits*) Miss Lupitya, when did this letter arrive?
VANA	Yesterday, very shortly after you left Bombay.
LANDAU	And you verified it?
VANA	We cabled Cooper, Cooper and Hill immediately. Their reply is attached to the letter there.
LANDAU	Yes, I've noted that. And the photostat of the Codicil.
VANA	This morning, Mrs Horrocks flew in from London, and we took the first available flight up to Janakpur.
JEREMY	Any chance of you publishing this information?
LANDAU	(*facing brothers*) It appears that a Codicil to Lord Rothbury's Will has come into the possession of Cooper, Cooper and Hill. I have a photostat here, and if the information in this letter is borne out, this tea estate will have a new Manager as from today.

MARTIN	What the hell are you talking about?
LANDAU	Lord Rothbury has stipulated that, although this estate is bequeathed to Lady Eppingham, it will be managed by Mrs Beatrice Horrocks.
JEREMY	What?
LANDAU	And she is to live here as one of the family.
MARTIN	Why on earth should he drag in a complete stranger?
LANDAU	(*rises*) Mrs Horrocks is not a complete stranger.
MARTIN	She is to us.
LANDAU	But not to the late Lord Rothbury. She is, in fact, his daughter.
JEREMY	What?
MARTIN	He hasn't got another daughter. Aunt Hester's the only one.
JEREMY	That's right. No brothers or sisters. Nobody.
LANDAU	Mrs Horrocks is Lord Rothbury's illegitimate daughter.

(RAHMU *enters to L. of doors.* HOUSEBOY *follows with her case.* BEATRICE HORROCKS *enters breezily C. She is aged about fifty and, although a good deal younger than* AUNTIE, *looks exactly like her.* BEATRICE *is full of bonhomie, a bustling Yorkshire lady. She wears a coat over her flowered dress, and a straw hat with a profusion of fruit on the top.*)

BEATRICE	I'm sorry. I can't wait in that taxi any longer. Where's the little girl's room?

(*She beams round at everybody. They all gape at her as*)

THE CURTAIN FALLS

The arrival of Beatrice Horrocks

Beatrice Horrocks

Scene Two

The same. Next morning. BEATRICE *is up a ladder D.L. taking down curtains. On the verandah are two tin baths.*

BEATRICE   (*unpinning curtain, and dropping it to floor. To herself*) Filthy, absolutely filthy. Only the aristocracy could put up with dirt like this. (*Turning to rhino's head on wall, and patting it.*) And you're looking a bit mangy and all, Tiddles. Never mind, I'll give you a shampoo later. (*Taking duster from apron.*) Now then, let's have a see.

(RAHMU *enters on verandah with letters*)

(*dusting above curtain rail*) Boy, they could grow radishes on top of here.

RAHMU   (*seeing* BEATRICE) Memsahib!

BEATRICE   (*slipping on ladder*) Ooh! Oh, you great daft bat!

RAHMU   (*placing letters on drinks cupboard*) What is Memsahib doing?

BEATRICE   Riding my bike. What does it look like?

RAHMU   (*cross to R. of ladder*) What has happened to the curtains?

BEATRICE   I'm giving them a damn good scrub. I shouldn't think you've had these down for a while.

RAHMU   They have not been touched since 1952.

BEATRICE   No, that's what it looks like.

RAHMU   But Memsahib should not be undertaking these menial tasks. This is done by Houseboys.

BEATRICE   Not very well, by the looks of it.

RAHMU   If Lady Eppingham sees what you are doing, she will go mad.

BEATRICE   Bit late for that I would have thought. (*Holding out her hand.*) Give us your hand. I'm coming down.

RAHMU	(*stepping back*) Memsahib, it is not permitted.
BEATRICE	Oh, come on darling. It's only my hand I'm offering you.
RAHMU	(*starting to go*) First I must go and put on my gloves.
BEATRICE	We haven't got time for all that caper. Cop hold before I break my neck. (*Puts duster in apron.*) ●
	(RAHMU *covers his hand with his sash. Steps forward, and helps her down.*)
	Now, that was all quite painless, wasn't it? (BEATRICE *picks up curtain, and takes out hooks.*)
RAHMU	I am afraid Memsahib does not understand our customs out here, but she will learn.
BEATRICE	If there's any learning to be done, it'll be done by you lot.
RAHMU	Our way of life goes back many hundreds of years. It may seem strange to the Memsahib but we have very definite rules to abide by. In my religion, I must show humility, respect and reverence.
BEATRICE	(*handing curtain to* RAHMU) Right. You can start by reverencing these then. Go on. Give them a good shake out on the balcony. I'll just put these back in the conservatory.
	(RAHMU *protests but goes out D.L.*)
	(*picking up ladder and crossing to verandah*) Aren't any of the family up yet? (*She rests the ladder on the verandah rail.*)
RAHMU	(*entering*) At eight o'clock in the morning? Certainly not.
BEATRICE	What about my sister?
RAHMU	(*holding curtain out on arms*) Lady Eppingham will be sleeping in this morning. She and Sir Harry are lunching at Government House.

BEATRICE	There is no Sir Harry.
RAHMU	There is no Government House either, but — (*He shrugs.*)
BEATRICE	Oh, I see. Bung it in that bath, dear.
RAHMU	Memsahib?
BEATRICE	Get stuck in, Gunghadin.
RAHMU	But Memsahib —
BEATRICE	Oh, don't tell me water's against your religion too? (*She dumps the curtains into the bath.*)
RAHMU	But Memsahib, I am not Dhobi Wallah.
BEATRICE	Dhobi what?
RAHMU	Dhobi — laundry. We have special houseboy for doing this.
BEATRICE	(*washing curtain*) I see, like the one who does the dusting?
RAHMU	Yes, yes.
BEATRICE	(*stopping her washing, and rolling up* RAHMU's *sleeves*) Come on, get your sleeves rolled up. We've got a lot of work to do.
RAHMU	(*faintly washing*) Lady Eppingham would never ask me to do anything like this.
BEATRICE	No, well she's not the only pebble on the beach now. As from last night, I'm the Manageress round here.
RAHMU	(*looking at her*) What about Martin Sahib?
BEATRICE	Oh, don't worry about him. I'll find him plenty do to.
RAHMU	Yes, Memsahib.
BEATRICE	(*stopping her work*) I say, isn't it marvellous. Two days ago Halifax, yesterday morning Bombay, and now here I am dhobi wallering in yankie-poo!

RAHMU	Janakpur.
BEATRICE	(*washing again*) Oh, yes.
RAHMU	It is long distance to travel.
BEATRICE	It is just to wash a pair of curtains!
RAHMU	(*stops washing, and looks at her*) The Memsahib has made this long journey just to wash the curtains?
BEATRICE	That was a joke. Have you ever been to Halifax?
RAHMU	Ali...?
BEATRICE	— Fax. Halifax, West Yorkshire.
RAHMU	No.
BEATRICE	It's in the north of England. You sure you never been there?
RAHMU	No, never.
BEATRICE	I could have sworn I've seen you down the Bradford Road.
RAHMU	Many of my country men are now emigrating to England.
BEATRICE	You can say that again. They're changing our whole way of life. Even our Baked Beans have been curried. Oh, look at the muck that's come out. And that's only after one quick dip.

(*They replace dirty tub with clean tub.*)

RAHMU	Memsahib does not like Indian Curry?

(*They start to rinse the curtain.*)

BEATRICE	Yes, it's alright I suppose.
RAHMU	It was on the menu last night.
BEATRICE	Was it?
RAHMU	But Memsahib did not come down.

BEATRICE	No, well, I thought it best to stay in bed after that rumpus when I arrived. (*Twisting curtain.*) Those two boys was in a right state and my poor sister mistaking me for Lady Mountbatten. What made her like that, Rahmu? Was it too much sun?
RAHMU	No. The Memsahib became like that after the accident.
BEATRICE	Oh, dear. What happened to her?
RAHMU	Nothing. It was Sir Harry. He was killed in a shooting accident.
BEATRICE	Oh, poor Hester.
RAHMU	No, no. She is not poor. She is great English Lady.
BEATRICE	Yes. It's hard to believe she and me had the same dad.
RAHMU	Very hard to believe.
BEATRICE	Have you got any family, Rahmu?
RAHMU	I had a sister, Memsahib, once.
BEATRICE	Oh, I am sorry, Rahmu.
	(*They start to lift the curtain.*)
RAHMU	Memsahib is pleased to be here in India?
BEATRICE	I'll say. I mean the East's so much more erotic, isn't it?
	(*They drape curtain over verandah rail.*)
MARTIN	(*off*) Rahmu! Rahmu! (*Entering.*) Rahmu, where the hell are you? What the devil are you doing?
BEATRICE	(*below* RAHMU) Good morning, Martin. We're dhobi wallering.
MARTIN	Never mind that. No one's had any breakfast yet.
BEATRICE	I have. Up with the lark, that's me.

MARTIN	(*curtly*) We don't have any larks out here, Mrs Horrocks.
BEATRICE	Well you've got something that makes a jolly old racket.
RAHMU	(*collecting letters from drinks cabinet*) Those are Kitehawks, Memsahib.
BEATRICE	Well, I was up with them then.
MARTIN	Rahmu, have there been any phone calls this morning?
RAHMU	Phone calls?
MARTIN	(*angrily*) Has anyone rung up from the station?
RAHMU	No, Sahib.
MARTIN	Damn.
RAHMU	Do you wish me to telephone?
MARTIN	No, just get the breakfast.
RAHMU	Yes, Sahib.
BEATRICE	Oh Rahmu. It doesn't matter about this morning dear, as I arrived a bit unexpected —
MARTIN	(*continuing to desk*) A bit?
BEATRICE	But for the future, I like to kick off with cornflakes and kippers. Got it? Kippers.
RAHMU	Kippers? (*He exits, muttering this word.*)
BEATRICE	He's an old scream, isn't he? Here, Martin, look at these. Haven't they come up a treat. I'm going to start on the cushion covers now. (*Cross to sofa.*)
MARTIN	I don't think that will be necessary, Mrs Horrocks. (*He picks up letters.*)
BEATRICE	Oh, it's no trouble. I don't mind pulling my weight. (*She goes through into drawing-room and starts to remove a loose cover.*) And for goodness sake, don't call me Mrs Horrocks. I'm Beatrice to my friends, but seeing as how we're related, you can call me Beattie.

MARTIN   (*going to telephone*) As your holiday here is
                likely to be brief I doubt if we shall become
                that intimate. (*Into phone.*) Get me Janakpur
                station.

BEATRICE   I'm not here on holiday, Martin. I'm here
                for keeps. (*Fiddling with cover tapes.*)
                Manageress. But don't you worry I won't
                make you redundant.

MARTIN   (*into phone*) No, I don't know the number.
                (*Smiling pleasantly at her.*) I think you'll find
                you're rather out of your depth here. It's
                not like England, you know.

BEATRICE   Good job, too. What with the weather
                freezing you and the Government squeezing
                you it's getting worse than Siberia. It hits
                the small man, you see. I was feeling the
                pinch in my haberdashers, I can tell you.

MARTIN   (*into phone*) Come on! Come on!

BEATRICE   (*she laughs*) There I've been selling Indian
                cottons for years, never dreaming I'd ever
                see where it come from.

MARTIN   Despite what you may have heard there's
                very little magic to be found here. The East
                can seem strangely hostile.

BEATRICE   I wouldn't say that, everyone's been most
                hospitable. And the main thing is I've got
                my family out here.

MARTIN   That hasn't actually been established yet.

BEATRICE   Do you know, Martin, that I didn't have a
                relative to my name after my George was
                taken? My late hubby that was, rest his
                soul. Apart from Lord Rothbury, that is,
                and I didn't know about him until after
                he'd snuffed it. (*She exits with loose covers
                D.L.*)

MARTIN	(*on phone*) Hullo… yes, has the Calcutta train arrived yet? What? What do you mean, delayed at Patna? How long a delay?
	(BEATRICE *re-enters without the covers.*)
BEATRICE	I was advertised for in the papers. Ooh, it were right exciting.
MARTIN	(*into phone*) No, I'll ring later. (*He puts the phone down and sits.*)
BEATRICE	Not that I saw it of course, 'cos I was stock-taking at the time. (*She picks up the elephant from the table.*) Hey, I've got one like that. My George won it on the hoop-la.
MARTIN	That, Mrs Horrocks, is real ivory.
BEATRICE	Oh, Martin, you'll have to take me round an ivory mine. (*She replaces it.*)
	(MARTIN *sits and opens letters.*)
	So there I was serving in my shop that day, when in comes my friend Edie Chalk, you know, Edie Chalk from Halifax. Well, she showed me this cutting and said I'd hear something to my advantage if I contacted this Cooper Cooper lot. You know, I nearly didn't. (*Dusting the drinks cupboard.*) Well, they were ever so nice to me when I went to see them. I was quite surprised. Gave me a lovely pot of tea, and then old Mr Cooper, he explained it all to me so nice. Mr Cooper senior, that is. Oh, he's a real love. Beautiful silvery sideboards. Oh, he does suit the part well. (*She turns and sees the rhinoceros head of the wall.*) Oh, the size of it. (*She laughs.*) He must have been going like a bomb when he hit that wall. (*Laughs more, then sits L. of* MARTIN, *who does not see the joke.*) Don't you get it Martin? Don't you? Oh, my George would of. He would have killed himself. Now where was I? Oh yes, well Mr Cooper said there was this letter

waiting my perusal at Barclays Bank, Pall
Mall, which couldn't be opened by anyone
but me. So, before you could say Jack
Robinson we was all in the Manager's
office, up to our eyeballs in tea again.
Well, my Mr Cooper had a bit of a natter
with the Bank Manager and then in comes
this Chief Cleric with a deed box. Oh,
Martin, it made me feel ever so funny when
they opened it and I see this envelope all
covered in Lord Rothbury's handwriting.
Addressed to me it was. Mrs B. Horrocks,
née Starling. Starling, that was my father,
well, what I'd always took to be my father.
He was Lord Rothbury's Butler. Anyway,
he opened this envelope, and do you know
what was inside?

MARTIN   No.

BEATRICE   A Codicil to the will. I don't suppose you
even know what a Codicil is, do you, dear?
(MARTIN *goes to speak.*) Well, a Codicil, dear,
is an adhesive to the Will. And also in the
envelope was this letter, addressed to me by
Lord Rothbury, my own illegitimate father.
(*She blows her nose to hide a tear.*)

(RAHMU *and* HOUSEBOY *enter with breakfast
tray.*)

RAHMU   Your breakfast, Sahib, for you and Master
Jeremy.

MARTIN   Oh, just put it down there.

(RAHMU *tells the boy in Hindustani to put it on
table.*)

BEATRICE   Rahmu, What time do the workers clock
on?

RAHMU   Clock on?

BEATRICE   Start work, love.

RAHMU   Already they are out in the fields. Work for
them begins at daybreak.

BEATRICE	Daybreak?
RAHMU	Yes. They are having to start early because they cannot work once the sun is getting too hot.
BEATRICE	Oh, I see, yes. I was forgetting. Oh, well, in that case, I think it's only fair if we all kick off at dawn.
	(RAHMU *takes newspaper to desk. Then crosses to gun cabinet.*)
MARTIN	Do you?
BEATRICE	Yes, I do, Martin. If I'm taking over here, I want to make sure that the family sets a proper example. And I know workers. I've had some. Who keeps an eye on them?
MARTIN	I do.
BEATRICE	Well, you can't keep an eye on them if you're snoring asleep in bed, can you Martin? Somebody might be diddling the estate left, right and centre.
	(JEREMY *enters wearing a dressing-gown.* RAHMU *steps in, holds chair.*)
BEATRICE	Oh, good morning, Wee willie winkle.
JEREMY	Morning Beattie, old love. Grub up, Rahmu? Good.
BEATRICE	(*crosses to between them, and pours coffee for* JEREMY) Bit early for lunch, isn't it?
JEREMY	You'll get used to us, Beattie.
BEATRICE	You take it black, I suppose?
JEREMY	Yes, thank you, Beattie.
BEATRICE	I've been telling your big brother there's going to be some changes round here.
JEREMY	How's that?
MARTIN	We're all getting up at dawn for one thing.
JEREMY	Good God.

BEATRICE	No, it's the only way to run a business, Jeremy. I think you've been a bit laxidasical with your staff here. I can just imagine what they're up to out there, with your Typhoo Tips I can hear them saying it, 'one tea leaf for Lady Eppingham, two tea leaves for me.' (JEREMY *grins as* MARTIN *looks away.*) It's quite easy you know. Why, I've had girls working for me, butter wouldn't melt in their mouths. (*She spreads butter on toast.*) That still hasn't stopped them walking out of the shop at 5.30 with two dozen reels of cotton stuffed up their knickers.
MARTIN	We can answer for our employees, thanks all the same.
JEREMY	In any case, I think they'd look a bit conspicuous walking out with a sack of tea up their dhoti.
BEATRICE	(*to* RAHMU) What's a dhoti?
RAHMU	(*stepping forward*) This is worn by Hindu men. It is a long piece of cloth with ornamented borders. It is tucked in at the waist, after passing round the loins and between the legs.
BEATRICE	Cheeky monkey. I think perhaps you're right, Jeremy. It don't sound at all the place for a sack of tea.
JEREMY	No.
BEATRICE	But there are other ways and means though—
MARTIN	You don't know the first thing about the organisation of a tea estate.
BEATRICE	No, granted Martin, I don't, but I can soon learn. After all, there's not that much difference between tea and drapery. It's all business, profit and loss. In the end, my accountant was coming to me for advice. Oh yes, that's one of the main reasons, why

my dad – er – Lord Rothbury denominated me for the job. He said it in that letter, he wasn't at all happy about the way business had been dropping off.

(MARTIN *bangs teacup*)

No offence meant to you Martin, and none taken I hope, but if there is any inefficiency I shall soon put my finger on it. (*Taking off apron and crossing to verandah.*) Rahm. I say, Rahm. I want you to escort me round the estate, love, so that I can have a natter with the peasants. (MARTIN *looks at her strangely.*) You can't beat the personal touch.

(*They exit to verandah, with* RAHMU *looking most unhappy.*)

JEREMY	Well, she's a charming turn-up for the books, isn't she?
MARTIN	Blasted woman!
JEREMY	Not your type?
MARTIN	She's catching the first train out of here.
JEREMY	From what I gather she intends to stay. At least she'll be company for Auntie.
MARTIN	Since when have you been concerned for the old girl's welfare?
JEREMY	As from now. I'm going to be a model nephew. Pander to her every whim. After all, we don't want to give her any reason to change her Will before Carradine gets here, do we?
MARTIN	If he ever does. (*Crosses towards drinks.*)
JEREMY	If he doesn't I'm going to have to make those arrangements of my own.
MARTIN	If you interfere in this I'll —
JEREMY	(*laughs*) No you won't. You pay people to do that for you. Like Carradine. (*Getting a new thought.*) He's ringing from the station isn't he?

MARTIN	Yes, when he arrives. God, I can't wait for it to be over. Then, with Auntie out of the way, I get power of attorney and sell for 100,000.
JEREMY	If you play your cards right I reckon you'd get 150,000 for this place.
MARTIN	How?
JEREMY	By throwing in Mrs Horrocks as lot number thirteen.
	(VANA enters U.C. JEREMY *rises*. MARTIN *faces her*.)
VANA	Good morning, gentlemen.
MARTIN	Good morning, my dear.
JEREMY	Good morning. (*Sits*.)
MARTIN	Have you had your breakfast yet?
VANA	No. Just black coffee. That is quite sufficient.
MARTIN	You're not slimming surely?
VANA	Yes.
MARTIN	Well, from what I can see, which is all too little, I would say you had a perfect figure.
VANA	(*stepping away*) Thank you.
JEREMY	Tell me, Miss Lupitya. Do you go for that subtle sophisticated approach?
VANA	A compliment is always most acceptable. You have a very attractive home here.
JEREMY	You don't have to return the compliment.
VANA	No, I mean it. There is a great deal of charm.
MARTIN	Yes, the old-world variety.
VANA	You should not despise the past, Mr Eppingham.
MARTIN	I don't. I'd rather not live in a morgue, that's all.

JEREMY	Don't worry. If Mrs Horrocks has her way, we'll have a neon sign over the gate, and bingo every Friday. (*Rises with cup of coffee and sits at desk. Reads newspaper.*)
VANA	(*laughing*) Oh, yes. Mrs Horrocks is quite a character. She made our plane journey from Bombay most enjoyable.
MARTIN	(*sarcastically*) I'm sure she was the life and soul of the party.
VANA	Indeed she was.
MARTIN	Stupid woman.
VANA	She may give the impression that she is naive, Mr Eppingham, but my instinct tells me that she is a very shrewd lady.
MARTIN	Is that so?
VANA	Oh yes. It is not unusual for it to cost the traveller to India a small fortune in porter's tips.
JEREMY	You're not joking.
VANA	However, I accompanied Mrs Horrocks from Bombay to Calcutta and from there to Janakpur and I found it a revelation in economics.
JEREMY	Tight-fisted, is she?
VANA	Not at all. But her lack of knowledge of our currency caused such confusion with the porters that she ended up with a handsome profit. (*She laughs.*) It would be difficult to believe, were it not for the striking facial resemblance, that Mrs Horrocks and Lady Eppingham were sisters.
MARTIN	Half-sisters. And even that remains to be proved.
VANA	Surely there is no doubt about it?
MARTIN	Well I doubt it for one.

VANA	(*stepping to* MARTIN) Come now, Mr Eppingham, you would not doubt the veracity of my client?
JEREMY	Your turn, Martin.
MARTIN	(*crosses to* JEREMY *at desk*) Look, why don't you go and get dressed. We don't want you lounging about like that.
JEREMY	Worry not. I'll be ready by the the time Dr Carradine gets here.
VANA	(*turning*) Carradine?
MARTIN	(*warily*) Yes.
VANA	Dr Carradine?
MARTIN	Yes. Why?
VANA	Oh. Is he a family friend?
JEREMY	(*enjoying the dangerous situation*) Hardly.
MARTIN	(*obscuring* JEREMY) It's a professional visit. He has this delightful nursing home up in the hills. Very exclusive.
JEREMY	And expensive.
	(MARTIN *glares at him.*)
VANA	I do not think it could be the same one.
MARTIN	Oh?
VANA	A Dr Carradine figured in one of my early court cases. From what I remember he was a most unsavoury character. (*She sits on sofa.*)
JEREMY	(*grinning at* MARTIN) Couldn't be the same one. This one can't do enough for you — isn't that so, Martin?
MARTIN	Go on. Get out of here.
	(*The door opens.* HOUSEBOY *enters with hatbox, followed by* AUNTIE.)
AUNTIE	Put it down there.

(HOUSEBOY *places hatbox on table by sofa,
removes elephant and places it above gramophone.*
MARTIN *moves to U.S. of desk.*)

JEREMY	Morning Auntie darling. (*He kisses her.*)
AUNTIE	Have you seen my sandwiches?
JEREMY	No, Auntie.
AUNTIE	That damn fool Rahmu must have packed them with my binoculars.
VANA	(*rising*) Good morning, Lady Eppingham.
AUNTIE	(*to* VANA) Ah, Lady Abercrombie. Do share our box at the races today.
MARTIN	(*to* AUNTIE) You're never down this early. You should still be in your bedroom.
AUNTIE	Not on the day of the races. (*To* VANA.) We've got Shalimar running in the Calcutta Gold Plate. If your husband has an extra hundred to spare, she's a very safe each way bet. He is still with us, I take it, your husband?
VANA	He's — I'm — we're not married.
AUNTIE	Too much of this living together. I don't believe in it.
MARTIN	Now come on back to bed, Aunt. You were going to rest today. Remember?
AUNTIE	(*sitting*) Not on the day of the races. (*To* VANA.) Shalimar was sired by Golden Miller. Or was it the other way round?
MARTIN	There are no races today, Aunt.
AUNTIE	No races?
MARTIN	No.
AUNTIE	They haven't been cancelled?
MARTIN	Yes, Aunt. Cancelled.
JEREMY	It's all that snow, old love.

AUNTIE	Don't talk rubbish, Jeremy. It's a beautiful sunny day. (*To* VANA.) I worry about him sometimes.
JEREMY	She's done it again.
MARTIN	(*taking hold of* AUNTIE) Now, come on —
AUNTIE	(*slapping his hand*) No, no, no. I'm going to show Lady Abercrombie my hat.
MARTIN	She doesn't want to see it.
AUNTIE	Of course she does. (*To* VANA.) You do, don't you?
VANA	Yes, please. Very much.
AUNTIE	There you are, clever clogs. (*To* VANA.) I find it difficult to get really angry with them, knowing their background. No parent. That's why they came to live with us. And my husband's worse than no use. He's so seldom here. It's my belief that Harry's got a love-nest in Darjeeling. The deceitful wretch.
JEREMY	Uncle wouldn't have anything like that.
AUNTIE	(*rising*) Have anything like what?
JEREMY	A love-nest in Darjeeling.
AUNTIE	I should think not. (*To* VANA, *stroking* JEREMY's *head.*) His uncle's been dead for years, Miss Lupitya. I don't know how to break it to him.
MARTIN	Now, please, Aunt —
AUNTIE	You are asking for a smacked bottie. Now, I am going to show Lady Abercrombie my hat before we go to the races. Don't want to clash, do we? (*Taking hat out of box.*) There, I trust it's not too similar?
VANA	No – no.
AUNTIE	(*putting on hat, facing* JEREMY) Let me have your opinion on it.

JEREMY	(*to* AUNTIE) That's lovely, Auntie.
AUNTIE	Yes, Martin?
MARTIN	Very nice.
AUNTIE	(*to* VANA) And you, my dear?
VANA	Absolutely charming.
AUNTIE	Thank you. (*As she replaces it in hatbox.*) Personally, I think it's bloody awful. (*Crosses to table and rings bell.*) Oh, come on, Rahmu. (*She rings the bell again. Telephone rings.*) What an extraordinary thing.
	(JEREMY *crosses to telephone and lifts receiver.* AUNTIE *picks up a piece of toast.*)
JEREMY	0343...yes. Eppingham speaking...could you speak up? I can't quite hear you.
MARTIN	Who is it?
JEREMY	Long distance, Patna.
MARTIN	(*taking telephone*) Give it to me. Hullo...Hullo?
AUNTIE	(*to* VANA) We don't know anyone called Long Distance Patna, do we?
VANA	It's the town of Patna.
AUNTIE	Ah, yes. Pretty place. I once played croquet there.
MARTIN	Who?...Haven't you left yet?... What?...How long a delay...That's no good. Could be weeks. I want you here today...
AUNTIE	Is that the Viceroy? (*Offers toast to* VANA.) Want a nibble?
MARTIN	Well there's nothing wrong with the weather here in Janakpur.
AUNTIE	Apart from a little snow.
MARTIN	It's imperative...What?...Hullo...Hullo? (*Replaces receiver.*) Carradine can't make it.

JEREMY	Why not?
MARTIN	The rains have started. He won't risk the journey.
AUNTIE	Who's Carradine?
MARTIN	Never mind.
AUNTIE	But I do mind. He could have joined our party at the races. Ring him back. Say I insist. He's no relation to that doctor who came here once, is he? Didn't like him. What was his name now? (*She laughs.*) You know, when you get to my age you tend to forget people's names, Lady Carradine.
VANA	I think you're quite remarkable.
AUNTIE	No. I've had a splendid life and if the next one is half as exciting, I can't wait. (*To* JEREMY.) Go and get dressed Jeremy, and don't forget to brush your hair. (*Rises and rings bell.*)
JEREMY	Yes, Auntie. (*He exits.*)
MARTIN	Come on, Rahmu. (*To* AUNTIE.) You've already rung that thing.
AUNTIE	Have I? Has he been?
MARTIN	No.
AUNTIE	I want my breakfast. (*Sits.*)
MARTIN	You'll have to wait. He's showing Mrs Horrocks round the estate.
AUNTIE	Mrs Who?
	(MARTIN *gives up and crosses onto verandah.*)
VANA	Mrs Horrocks. The lady with whom I arrived last night.
AUNTIE	Yes, of course. You mean my half-sister, Beatrice.
VANA	(*rising*) You knew her, then?

AUNTIE	Not until last night. I was overjoyed to meet her. She went straight to bed.
VANA	She was very tired after her journey.
AUNTIE	It's only twenty minutes from Janakpur.
VANA	She's come from Halifax!
AUNTIE	Well, half an hour, then. Most extraordinary her turning up like that. She's a chip off the old block. We shall have many a happy hour together. I find her a little difficult to follow. I suppose she is English, isn't she?
VANA	Er — yes.
AUNTIE	(*rising*) What a pity we didn't meet sooner. She could have been my bridesmaid. (*Leading* VANA *to sofa. She sits*) Good God, we've been burgled. The cushions! Surely you've seen it. Peacocks on Pineapples. Go and fetch Rahmu for me, quickly.
VANA	(*rises*) I'm sure nobody would actually steal your cushions.
AUNTIE	Don't you believe it. They'd take the curtains if you gave them half a chance. (*Sees they are missing.*) Good God, they have. (*Crosses back to table for bell.*) Rahmu, Rahmu, quickly. Fetch him.
	(VANA *exits.* AUNTIE *crosses to verandah, ringing bell.*)
	Rahmu, Rahmu.
MARTIN	What is it?
AUNTIE	You're not Rahmu, are you? We've been burgled. They've taken the curtains.
MARTIN	Mrs Horrocks is washing them. They're out here, drying.
AUNTIE	Would you believe it? All I asked her to do was to shorten my dress for the Viceroy's ball and she takes a liberty like this.

(LANDAU *enters.*)

And, so you're back from Darjeeling, are you? (*Gives him bell.*)

LANDAU   Darjeeling?

AUNTIE   Yes. You didn't know I'd followed you, did you? I know all about that native girl, you deceitful wretch.

LANDAU   I haven't got a girl in Darjeeling.

AUNTIE   Oh, well, we'll have to see what we can do for you, Mr Landau.

LANDAU   (*gets a grip on himself*) Is Mr Eppingham down yet?

AUNTIE   Which Mr Eppingham? Martin or Jeremy?

LANDAU   Either will do.

AUNTIE   (*calls*) Martin — the doctor's here to see you.

MARTIN   Doctor?

LANDAU   It is I, Mr Eppingham.

MARTIN   Oh. (*He goes up steps and onto verandah.*)

AUNTIE   (*sitting*) Surely you recognise Mr Landau. He's been here long enough. (*Offering* LANDAU *toast.*) Do you want some breakfast?

LANDAU   I've already had it, thank you.

AUNTIE   You're lucky. I'm absolutely starving. (*She marches* LANDAU *to the sofa.*) Now, before you go, I want you to do me a little favour.

LANDAU   Little favour?

                (MARTIN *stirs on verandah.*)

AUNTIE   Shh. I want you to make an alteration to my Will.

LANDAU	Oh, certainly. I hope it's not too complicated.
AUNTIE	Good gracious, no. I merely want to leave everything I have to my beloved sister, Beatrice.
LANDAU	Are you sure you mean that?
AUNTIE	Mean what?
LANDAU	That you want her to inherit the estate.
AUNTIE	Certainly. (*Looping arms.*) We've no children of our own, have we, darling?
LANDAU	(*very embarrassed*) Er — no. What about your nephews?
AUNTIE	Vultures both of them. Don't give a fig for me. But with Beatrice, it's a different matter.
LANDAU	Perhaps we could get it done right away.
AUNTIE	You think so?
LANDAU	Certainly. Where is the document?
AUNTIE	I haven't the faintest idea.
LANDAU	Well, if you could find it before lunch —
AUNTIE	Anything's possible.
	(JEREMY *enters.*)
JEREMY	Morning, Mr Landau. Sleep well?
LANDAU	As well as I ever do in a strange bed.
AUNTIE	Ah, I knew you'd spent the night in Darjeeling.
JEREMY	Been a naughty boy again, have you?
AUNTIE	No worse than you. Let me see your hands.
JEREMY	(*showing them*) They're quite clean, Auntie.
AUNTIE	Yes. They wouldn't be if you worked harder. (*Rising with* LANDAU, *crosses to guns.*) Come along, Doctor. We've just time for a little duck shooting before lunch.

LANDAU	Er — I don't shoot.
AUNTIE	But you should. I'm going to teach you. (*Takes out gun.*)
LANDAU	Isn't there something else we should be doing?
AUNTIE	What? Oh well — if that's how you feel — to hell with the duck shooting!
	(*They exit.*)
JEREMY	(*spotting* MARTIN *on verandah*) Hullo. Did you hear that?
MARTIN	Yes, and a lot more.
JEREMY	Oh? You know, I have an idea we might be in line for a new uncle as well.
MARTIN	We're in line for nothing. She's changing the Will.
JEREMY	Good-O. You mean contesting it?
MARTIN	Not Rothbury's. Her own. She's leaving the lot to Mrs Horrocks.
	(JEREMY *hesitates then laughs, crosses to drinks and takes peanuts.*)
JEREMY	Poor Aunt Hester. Now, she's only got herself to blame. Doesn't leave us much option, does it?
MARTIN	If only Carradine could have got here today.
JEREMY	(*viciously*) If, if, if. (*Grinning.*) There's no one to help you now, except me and a friend of mine.
MARTIN	Friend? What friend?
JEREMY	(*crosses to door*) Just a friend. (*He exits.*)
MARTIN	(*starting to follow*) Jeremy —
	(RAHMU *and* VANA *enter on verandah. He is agitated.*)
RAHMU	Martin Sahib, Sahib.

MARTIN	(*turning*) Yes?
RAHMU	Sahib, it is Memsahib Horrocks.
MARTIN	What about her?
RAHMU	It is most disturbing. She has engaged herself in coversation with some of the workers and already she has promised them a hundred per cent increase in their wages.
MARTIN	Oh, my God. I'll deal with her later. (*He exits.*)
VANA	Rahmu, I think you will find that Mrs Horrocks has a most individual approach to economics.
RAHMU	She will have everyone out on strike if she is not careful.
VANA	(*to* RAHMU) No doubt Mr Eppingham will fire any troublemakers. That soon brings the others into line.
RAHMU	That is what they told Memsahib Horricks they were afraid of.
VANA	Ah.
RAHMU	Then she told them to try collective bargaining.
	(BEATRICE *appears on verandah, with* HOUSEBOY.)
BEATRICE	Come on, dear. Don't be shy. Come along in, my old china. (*They enter.*)
RAHMU	China?
BEATRICE	Do you know what this little lad's been telling me? He hasn't had a day off in months.
RAHMU	There is a very good reason for this.
BEATRICE	What's that?
RAHMU	He is not entitled to one. (*Taking boy by ear, throws him out of door. Returns to R. of* BEATRICE.) And if I catch you talking to Memsahib again you won't get a day off at all.

BEATRICE	Rahmu, you mustn't treat people like that.
VANA	Our ways are not your ways, Mrs Horrocks.
BEATRICE	If that kid had been working in one of our docks, you'd have had the pickets at the gates by now.
RAHMU	Labour is plentiful here.
BEATRICE	That's no reason to take advantage of the situation. They've been telling me about their contracts.
RAHMU	Contracts?
BEATRICE	For them little tea pluckers.
RAHMU	But there are no contracts.
BEATRICE	That's what I mean. (*Crosses to* VANA.) You get some drawn up, love, and we'll dish them out tomorrow.
VANA	It's a pity you did not arrive two hundred years ago.
BEATRICE	Yes, well I've been busy. And what about National Health, Social Clubs, Luncheon Vouchers?
RAHMU	We are not having Social Clubs.
BEATRICE	Well, where do you play your darts and bingo?
VANA	They do not go in for those pastimes here.
BEATRICE	No 'middle for diddle', 'legs eleven'?
RAHMU	(*uncomprehending*) No, no. We are not having eleven legs.
BEATRICE	Right. Starting Monday, we're going to convert one of them warehouses. With a special treat of a Saturday — old time dancing. Then of course there's the annual outing to the seaside.
VANA	I am afraid the nearest seaside is four hundred miles away.

BEATRICE	Well, we'll take them up into the hills then.
VANA	The Himalayas?
BEATRICE	(*crosses to door*) Yes, they'll do. Anyway, you must have plenty of local beauty spots. Take 'em up the Khyber Pass? (*She exits.*)
VANA	I'm rather sorry I won't be here to see the results of her efforts.
RAHMU	I only hope Memsahib Horrocks is still here.
VANA	I don't understand.
RAHMU	If Memsahib Horrocks stays, she will be in danger.
VANA	I think Mrs Horrocks can take care of herself, Rahmu.
RAHUM	*Grave* danger. I have seen a sign in the sky. It means an evil spirit in Janakpur. It comes with the stranger.
VANA	(*to herself*) Dr Carradine.
RAHMU	Carradine?
VANA	(*turns to* RAHMU) It's all right, Rahmu. The doctor is not calling to see Mrs Horrocks. And in any case I believe she would be more than a match for him.
RAHMU	No, no I was not referring to Dr Carradine. He is no stranger to Janakpur. No, the evil spirit has already arrived. It is Landau Sahib. Before the day is out the gods will take their vengeance. We shall see!
VANA	(*sharply*) That is enough, Rahmu.
RAHMU	(*angrily*) Ever since your Landau Sahib arrived there had been discord in the house. He is the evil one.
VANA	Rahmu! For your own sake, be quiet.
RAHMU	(*levelly*) He is the one.

VANA	(*quietly*) Mr Landau was not the only stranger to arrive here.
RAHMU	Who else?
VANA	Myself.
RAHMU	(*eyeing her*) Are you a stranger, Miss Lupitya?

(*There is a gun shot.* LANDAU *enters hurriedly, pointing off stage but unable to speak. Then he,* RAHMU *and* VANA *go off.*)

CURTAIN

ACT TWO

Scene One

The same. A few minutes later. AUNTIE *is sitting in the armchair with the gun in her lap.* VANA *is waving a bottle of smelling salts under* AUNTIE'S *nose.* LANDAU *is pouring a brandy.*

AUNTIE	(*sitting on sofa, holding gun in L. hand*) Stop fussing with that stuff and hurry up with my brandy, Doctor. (VANA *removes smelling salts.*) What's that you've got there?
VANA	The smelling salts.
AUNTIE	Well, give them to me then. (*She takes them.*)
LANDAU	(*turning at drinks*) You're quite sure you weren't injured at all?
AUNTIE	I don't think so. But when you get to my age you can't tell the difference between lumbago and buck-shot. It certainly put the wind up my poor sister. (*To* VANA.) What was it she said she was going to do in the fields?
VANA	(*taking salts*) Organise the elevenses.
AUNTIE	Oh, are they playing cricket?
LANDAU	(*turning at drinks with glass*) It's a modern colloquialism. (*Handing drink over her L. shoulder.*) Would you care to drink this?
AUNTIE	(*taking it*) Try and stop me. (*To* VANA. LANDAU *turns back to drinks to put bottle away.*) This is the stuff to give the troops, Lady Abercrombie. Don't put the bottle away yet, Doctor. And get rid of this thing. (*Indicating gun.*) I don't think I shall shoot any more today.
LANDAU	(*taking gun, crosses to R. of sofa*) Very wise.
AUNTIE	I'd no idea it was loaded. What did I bring down?
LANDAU	Very little apart from the ceiling.

AUNTIE	Got a kick like a mule. Why weren't you there to catch me, Harry?
LANDAU	Don't you think we should forget the shooting incident now?
AUNTIE	Oh, but I have. I've forgotten all about it, Doctor. It happened so many years ago. When are you going to make an honest woman of Lady Abercrombie?
	(LANDAU *and* VANA *exchange looks.*)
LANDAU	I — er — I thought I'd leave it until after I'd amended your Will.
AUNTIE	Very good of you to put it off on my account.
LANDAU	(*crosses to cabinet*) Don't you think we should be looking for the document?
AUNTIE	(*rising*) What a very good idea. (LANDAU *puts gun away.*) You have a good hunt for it in here while I have a rest before the journey. (*Gives glass to* VANA.) It's bound to be somewhere in the house. We've never lived anywhere else. Have a look in that work basket, my dear.
VANA	Certainly. What for?
	(LANDAU *crosses to L. of door*)
AUNTIE	My Will of course.
	(VANA *crosses to workbasket U.L.* AUNTIE *crosses away R.*)
	Now where's he got to? (*Turns to see* LANDAU.) Ah, Doctor, have you seen Mr Landau? (*Crosses to* LANDAU.) Tell him to come to my room. (*She exits.*)
LANDAU	I shan't be sorry when this visit's over.
VANA	(*teasing*) No — Doctor?
LANDAU	(*crosses to desk*) I don't know what to do. I really don't. (*Sits at desk.*)

VANA	(*crosses to table C, puts down work box and looks in it.*) Why are we looking for it?
LANDAU	Because Lady Eppingham wishes to amend it.
VANA	Really?
LANDAU	(*searching in drawers*) She's decided to leave everything to Mrs Horrocks instead of the two brothers. (*Continuing to search.*) If she doesn't know where it is, I really don't think we can be expected — (*Bangs a drawer shut.*) Whatever happens, Miss Lupitya, we're catching that train. I've wasted nearly three days away from the office as it is.
VANA	Perhaps we should fly back.
LANDAU	No thank you.
VANA	(*crosses back U.L. to put box back*) I think the quickest and simplest step would be to draw up a fresh one.
LANDAU	I would have serious qualms about that. The opening paragraph, 'I, Lady Eppingham, being of sound mind — '
	(LANDAU *opens another drawer and searches.*)
RAHMU	(*entering*) What is Sahib doing?
	(LANDAU *slams drawer shut and spins round to face* RAHMU.)
LANDAU	What do you want?
RAHMU	Has Sahib lost something?
LANDAU	Don't you usually knock before coming into a room?
RAHMU	I did not think there was anyone here. Perhaps I could help —
LANDAU	No.
VANA	It is all right, thank you, Rahmu. Just a letter belonging to Lady Eppingham.

RAHMU	(*to* VANA) Her Ladyship's correspondence is kept in the office. Shall I — ?
LANDAU	No. Getting damn close. Don't they have any fans here?
RAHMU	No, Sahib.
VANA	(*crosses to sofa and sits*) I think we could do with some iced water.
	(RAHMU *bows, and goes U.S.* BEATRICE *enters on verandah.*)
BEATRICE	Sweaty old day isn't it, Mr Landau?
LANDAU	(*rising*) Yes, indeed it is.
BEATRICE	(*holding out top of her dress*) We'll have to find the answer to this little lot, won't we?
LANDAU	Quite, quite.
RAHMU	I am getting some iced water.
BEATRICE	Oh, I don't fancy that down the front of me. (*She laughs.*) No, I see what you mean, dear. No, I fancy something a bit stronger. Got any Tizer?
RAHMU	Tizer?
BEATRICE	Tizer. Tizer the appetiser.
RAHMU	Happy tizer? We have Coca-Cola.
BEATRICE	Oh, well. Mix that with a bit of orange and a squirt of soda, and we'll have our own. (*Crosses to* VANA.) You'd like some Tizer, wouldn't you?
VANA	No, thank you.
BEATRICE	Oh, aren't you hot?
VANA	Not particularly.
BEATRICE	(*sitting on sofa*) Oh, I suppose wearing that Safari helps. (*Turns to* LANDAU.) You must be boiling in that suit.
LANDAU	No.

BEATRICE	Have you got a vest on? (*She tries to look.*)
LANDAU	No!
BEATRICE	Oh, that explains it. He's cheating. I'm still dressed for the English winter. Do you know, when I left Halifax, there was eighteen inches of icicle hanging off my overflow. There won't half be a dickens of a mess when that lot thaws. I should worry. I've sold it to some poor Pakistani. (*She laughs.*) Oh, I am sorry. You're not offended, I hope.
RAHMU	Certainly not. It is no more than they deserve.
BEATRICE	Eh? Oh yes, of course. I was forgetting. You lot don't hit it off together, do you? Colour problem, is it?
	(RAHMU's *smile vanishes.*)
RAHMU	(*turning to* BEATRICE) I will get your drink. (*To himself.*) Coca bloody Cola!
	(RAHMU *exits muttering.*)
BEATRICE	Isn't he touchy. What did I say?
LANDAU	Oh, nothing, Mrs Horrocks. Nothing.
VANA	It is a religious problem, Mrs Horrocks. Very complex.
BEATRICE	Oh?
VANA	The Pakistanis are Muslims.
BEATRICE	Oh, not C. of E. like you and me?
VANA	No.
LANDAU	(*sitting R. of table*) Well really —
VANA	As it happens, I am a Hindu.
BEATRICE	No, you're never. Well, it takes all sorts. (*Sits on sofa.*) I've no time for prejudice. I think all those who won't live and let live ought to be shot.

LANDAU	Yes, that should do it.
BEATRICE	I mean life isn't long enough.
VANA	No. We're none of us perfect.
BEATRICE	I mean here's me illegitimate, and you Indian, but we don't let that get us down.
VANA	To tell you the truth, Mrs Horrocks, my nationality has never embarrassed me.
BEATRICE	No, 'course not. We've got to rise above that sort of thing. I mean most people is just common or garden, but Miss Lupitya and me, well we've got a little bit something extra in life. Do you know, up to three days ago, every day was the same to me. I was one of your humdrum millions. Not any more. Now I wake up and I say, 'Beattie, you're unique. You're illegitimate.'
LANDAU	Yes, I can see that might be compensation.
BEATRICE	Well, it's more of a bonus in my particular case, 'cos I was sired by a nobleman.
VANA	Yes. That must have been a great surprise to you.
BEATRICE	Well, it was and it wasn't, if you get my meaning. Even as a little girl it would never have surprised me if I'd grown up to be a princess.

(RAHMU *and* HOUSEBOY *enter with Tizer.*)

'Cos I was brought up among the nobs, wasn't I? It was just one stately home after the other until I was thirteen, what with Mum and Dad being in service. Well, I say my dad, but I didn't know the rights of the matter then. I suppose, to put it tactfully, you could say that my father was noble enough to step in and foot the bill after Lord Rothbury had run up the account. (*She laughs, then notices the servants.*) Oh, hark at me, in front of the servants.

RAHMU	Your — er — Tizer, Memsahib.
BEATRICE	Oh, lovely.
RAHMU	Shall I have it put down here?
BEATRICE	No, we'll have it on the balcony. It doesn't seem quite so hot now.
RAHMU	I do not think that this is advisable, Memsahib. I fear the rains are coming.
LANDAU	Oh Lord. I thought it was clouding over.
BEATRICE	Oh well, a little shower will freshen things up nicely. Take it through, Rahmu.
	(RAHMU *and* HOUSEBOY *go onto verandah and arrange table and chairs. They also clear the remains of the washing scene.*)
VANA	I am afraid that sometimes our little showers can last as long as six weeks.
BEATRICE	How long?
LANDAU	(*rising*) It plays havoc with the trains. If it gets really bad it can wash the tracks away.
BEATRICE	Oh I can't believe that. Anyway, you should worry. Take an aeroplane.
LANDAU	In a raging storm?
BEATRICE	They fly over it.
LANDAU	They have to get through it first.
BEATRICE	Oh. You've got a funny tummy, have you?
LANDAU	Yes.
BEATRICE	Never mind. They keep you well supplied with paper bags. And all you have to do is —
LANDAU	Thank you, yes.
VANA	Mr Landau, why don't you ring the railway station at Janakpur. They will probably put your mind at ease.

BEATRICE	I can just imagine what they'd say at King's Cross if you rang them up and said, 'Looks like rain this morning. Got any line left between here and Cleethorpes?'
LANDAU	All the same, I think I will just check with the station and see what they say. May I use your telephone, Mrs Horrocks?
BEATRICE	Yes, of course you may. (*To* VANA.) I'll tell you what. If it really comes on to rain, we'll all sit round and watch the telly.
VANA	(*rising*) There is no television in Janakpur.
BEATRICE	No television? Not even B.B.C.?
VANA	Not even Delhi can transmit over the Himalayas.
LANDAU	(*into telephone*) Hullo...Hullo?
	(BEATRICE *and* VANA *start to cross to verandah.*)
VANA	We need many more transmitting stations.
BEATRICE	Cor, you'd think they'd be able to bounce it off one of them stalegmites up there.
	(BEATRICE *is on verandah, L. of* LANDAU.)
LANDAU	Hullo. Hullo.
BEATRICE	'Who's your lady friend.'
LANDAU	The phone's dead.
BEATRICE	Are you sure?
VANA	But Mr Eppingham was speaking on it only just now.
LANDAU	Well, it's dead now.
RAHMU	(*handing drink to* BEATRICE) Memsahib.
BEATRICE	Ta.
LANDAU	(*to* RAHMU) Did you know the confounded telephone was out of order?
RAHMU	No, Sahib.

BEATRICE	Here, let me try. (*Handing drink to* LANDAU.) Hold that Tizer. (*She takes telephone from* LANDAU.) Never mind Hullo, hullo? Can you hear me? You're quite right, dear. It's dead.
	(LANDAU *hands her back the drink and replaces telephone.*)
RAHMU	It is not unusual in the rainy season.
BEATRICE	You mean the wires is down.
LANDAU	I should never have sent that taxi away last night. I should have gone when I intended. (*Irritated, to* BEATRICE.) I would have, if you hadn't arrived.
BEATRICE	Oh, did you stop because of me? How nice. Come on, lets have our drinks on the verandah. I've never seen a tropical monsoon before.
LANDAU	(*to* RAHMU) Rahmu, is there another telephone in the house?
RAHMU	Yes, Sahib. There is extension on the upstairs landing.
LANDAU	Upstairs? Well, I think it might be advisable if I checked on that one. (*Crosses to door.*) I'll be back in a moment. (*He exits.*)
BEATRICE	Isn't he an old fidgetty britches. I say, is that Mr Landau married?
VANA	I'm afraid I don't know. I only joined the firm recently.
BEATRICE	I hope not. I wouldn't mind taking him on. I enjoy a challenge. (*They go onto verandah.*) Come on, let's get ourselves organised out here. Now sit down there, and we'll keep this chair for Mr Landau.
	(RAHMU *crosses to room and picks up telephone.* MARTIN *enters,* RAHMU *replaces receiver. He and* MARTIN *look at one another then* RAHMU *bows and exits.* MARTIN *crosses to desk and sits.*)

	Oh, we get a lovely view of the hills from here. You haven't touched your drink.
VANA	Yes, I've had a sip, thank you.
BEATRICE	Don't you like it?
VANA	I think perhaps you have to acquire a taste for it, or else be very thirsty.
BEATRICE	Well, I'm thirsty all right. (*She drinks.*) Ugh! Where's he dredged this lot up from? The Ganges? Ay-up, it's starting.

(*There is a flash of lightning.* JEREMY *enters on verandah with cardboard box about the size of a shoebox.*)

BEATRICE	Hullo, Jeremy.
JEREMY	Hullo, Beattie.
BEATRICE	Come to watch the fireworks?
JEREMY	Yes. It won't be long now either.
BEATRICE	Exciting, isn't it?
JEREMY	I suppose your first one is.
BEATRICE	It's better than Blackpool Illuminations.

(JEREMY *goes through into drawing-room.*)

JEREMY	Lost something?
MARTIN	I'm looking for that damn Will.
JEREMY	Don't bother.
MARTIN	It's not in the office. It must be in her room. If only that damned Carradine could have got here today, she'd have been carted off by now.
JEREMY	Well, he didn't, and she hasn't. (*He sits.*)

(MARTIN *starts to exits.*)

	Martin. I've got a present for her.
MARTIN	(*turning*) Present?
JEREMY	For our sakes, I think she ought to have it.

MARTIN	(*stepping in to above table*) What is it?
JEREMY	A little parting gift for Aunt Hester. I know you'll approve. I picked it up just now.
	(MARTIN *lifts lid, then closes it in horror. There is a flash of lightning.*)
MARTIN	You bloody fool. You know I can't stand those things.
JEREMY	Neither can Aunt Hester. One nip from our friend here, and she'll be saying, 'Move over Daddy, here I come.'
MARTIN	You're mad.
	(*There is a rumble of thunder.* LANDAU *enters and stops on seeing* MARTIN *and* JEREMY.)
LANDAU	That telephone doesn't work either. (*Crosses to verandah.*) The sooner we get our business wound up, Miss Lupitya, the sooner I can go.
BEATRICE	You're always wanting to go. There's nothing wrong with you, is there? Come on. Park it there, and wrap your gums round this. It'll cool you off.
LANDAU	Peculiar colour, isn't it?
	(RAHMU *enters.*)
RAHMU	Excuse me, Sahib.
MARTIN	What do you want?
RAHMU	Lady Eppingham wishes to see you, Sahib.
MARTIN	What for?
RAHMU	She would not tell me.
MARTIN	Yes — all right.
RAHMU	Very good, Sahib. Also she is thinking she has left her hatbox down here.
MARTIN	All right, all right. It's over there.
RAHMU	Thank you, Sahib (RAHMU *crosses to hatbox and picks it up.*)

JEREMY	(*suddenly*) Rahmu.
RAHMU	Sahib?
JEREMY	Don't bother. As Martin's going up, he'll take it. Won't you, Martin?
RAHMU	Very good, Sahib. (*Crosses in and places box on table.*) Memsahib would like it as soon as possible, Sahib.
JEREMY	Don't worry. She'll get it.
	(RAHMU *bows and exits.*)
	'Along came a spider and sat down beside her.'
	(*There is a flash of lightning.*)
	(*rising*) All right, Martin?
	(MARTIN *opens hatbox.* JEREMY *shakes his box and we catch a fleeting glimpse of a large black spider. It drops in.* MARTIN *closes lid quickly.*)
	Voila! It's all yours.
	(*A loud crash of thunder which brings the others into the room.*)
BEATRICE	Boy, that was close.
VANA	I think I will fetch my stole from upstairs. Mrs Horrocks, can I get you anything?
BEATRICE	I wouldn't mind a drop of brandy. My heart's going like a sledge-hammer. (*Taking* LANDAU*'s hand.*) Go on, you feel.
LANDAU	(*withdrawing hand*) I'll take your word for it.
BEATRICE	(*seeing hatbox*) Oh, what's that?
MARTIN	Lady Eppingham's hatbox.
BEATRICE	(*crosses to table*) Oh, isn't that a lovely bit of old leather? (*She picks it up.*)
MARTIN	(*freezing*) Put that down, Mrs Horrocks.

BEATRICE	Do you know, the last time I saw one of these was at Lane End Methodist Christmas Bazaar. I don't suppose you have them out here, bazaars…
LANDAU	Bazaar, Mrs Horrocks, is an Indian word.
BEATRICE	No. It's never? Well, live and learn.
MARTIN	(*trying desperately to be calm*) My aunt would like her hat, if you don't mind.
BEATRICE	Is there a hat in there? (*Crosses to table and puts box down. She opens it.*) Come on, let's have a see. Oh, that's all real silk. And that's only the lining. This must have cost a bob or two. I'd love a box like this to keep my bits and bobs in. (*She closes box.*)
MARTIN	(*grabs box from her*) We'll make you a present of this one, before you go back to Halifax.

(JEREMY *opens door.* MARTIN *exits.*)

BEATRICE	Isn't he a scream? The way he keeps on you'd think he wanted to get rid of his old auntie.

(VANA *enters, wearing a colourful stole.*)

Oh, that's beautiful, Miss Lupitya.

VANA	Thank you.

(JEREMY *closes door.*)

BEATRICE	In all my years in haberdashery, I never seen colours like that. I bet that were made in Hong Kong.
LANDAU	(*quickly*) Miss Lupitya, do you think we could attend to the matter in hand, without further interruptions.

(VANA *crosses to* LANDAU *and sits on sofa.*)

BEATRICE	(*stepping in*) You're finding it hard to get on with your soliciting today, aren't you?
LANDAU	Yes. But I intend to persevere.

BEATRICE	That's right. You press on regardless.
	(JEREMY *sits. There is a knock at the door.*)
BEATRICE	Come in.
	(RAHMU *enters with* HOUSEBOY.)
RAHMU	Excuse me, Memsahib.
BEATRICE	What is it, Squire?
RAHMU	May we clear away the drinks, please?
	(*There is a rumble of thunder.*)
BEATRICE	Yes, you may.
	(RAHMU *and* HOUSEBOY *cross to verandah.*)
LANDAU	Rahmu, can you show me where the office is?
RAHMU	Yes, Sahib. But in view of the rains I think you will need an umbrella.
LANDAU	Well, get one and be quick about it.
RAHMU	Yes, Sahib. (*He starts to go.*) Oh, forgive me, Sahib. I had forgotten. (*Takes out Will.*) Her Ladyship asked me to give you this but the storm is putting it out of my mind.
LANDAU	(*taking Will*) Ah! That'll save us valuable time.
RAHMU	Her Ladyship hopes she has caused you no inconvenience.
LANDAU	We had been looking for it down here.
RAHMU	She found it in her handbag. (*Goes onto verandah.*)
BEATRICE	What's that, then?
JEREMY	(*casually*) Looks like Auntie's Will, old love. Nothing going on is there, Landau?
LANDAU	Well — I — er believe your aunt is toying with the idea of making a slight amendment.

JEREMY	(*grinning*) Is she really?
RAHMU	I hope I did right in witnessing the alteration, Sahib.
	(JEREMY's *attitude changes as he realised the implication.*)
JEREMY	Alteration?
RAHMU	Yes, Sahib.
JEREMY	When?
RAHMU	About ten minutes ago. Her Ladyship called in the houseboy and myself.
LANDAU	Well, really, she might have —
RAHMU	I hope I have done nothing wrong, Sahib?
LANDAU	No, no, it's quite in order —
JEREMY	(*to* RAHMU) Get out of here!
RAHMU	But, Sahib —
JEREMY	(*screaming*) Out!
	(RAHMU *hurries out through verandah.* JEREMY *crosses to* LANDAU *and snatches* Will.) Let me see that.
LANDAU	(*snatching it back*) Give it to me, sir.
	(MARTIN *enters.*)
JEREMY	I am entitled to —
LANDAU	And I'm being paid to —
BEATRICE	What's all the fuss about?
	(MARTIN *puts hatbox on table. All turn to him.*)
BEATRICE	What's the matter with you? You look like the curse of the Mummy's tomb.
MARTIN	It's Aunt Hester.
BEATRICE	What?
MARTIN	She's dead.

BEATRICE	Well, here's a bloody fine how-do-you-do? (*She exits followed by* VANA *and* LANDAU.)
JEREMY	(*to* MARTIN) Do you know what you've done?
MARTIN	She was dead when I got there. Strangled.
	(*There is a flash of lightning followed by heavy thunder.*)

CURTAIN

Scene Two

A few moments later. JEREMY *is drinking.* MARTIN *is sitting on the settee. The drink has calmed* JEREMY *but* MARTIN *is very much on edge. The thunder is dying out.*

JEREMY	(*holding up decanter*) How about you?
	(MARTIN *shakes his head.*)
	You look as if you need it more than I do.
MARTIN	Her eyes were staring at me — it was hideous.
JEREMY	I've never seen anyone who's been strangled.
MARTIN	Nor had I. I don't want to see it again either. (*Miming it.*) The scarf was drawn so tight you could . . .
JEREMY	Take it easy.
MARTIN	Her face was twisted — blue.
JEREMY	(*chuckles*) So . . . er — somebody's read our thoughts.
MARTIN	(*looking hard at* JEREMY) Yes — somebody.
JEREMY	Well, I mean it wasn't you, was it?
MARTIN	No.
JEREMY	(*laughing*) And it wasn't me.
MARTIN	No?

(RAHMU *enters from behind French windows and walks along the balcony around to the verandah. He lets down the bamboo blinds and then collects the tray.* JEREMY *and* MARTIN *are talking through this.*)

JEREMY	Why should I?
MARTIN	I don't know.
JEREMY	It doesn't really matter who did.
MARTIN	(*after a slight pause*) You actually saw the Will?
JEREMY	Yes. Beattie Horrocks cops the lot. Beattie. (*He laughs.*)
MARTIN	It's not funny.
JEREMY	Mark you, with a bit of luck, whoever did it might carry on the good work.
MARTIN	How do you mean?
JEREMY	Give Beattie Horrocks the same treatment.
MARTIN	And if he — or she — doesn't?
JEREMY	There's an equally good solution. But I'm afraid it's up to you.
MARTIN	You don't think I'd be such a damn fool as to try that again. (*He indicates hatbox.*)
JEREMY	No. I don't mean our friend in here. There's something far more subtle and equally effective. You simply 'pop the question'.
MARTIN	What?
JEREMY	If you marry Beattie . . .
MARTIN	You *are* mad.
JEREMY	Listen, if you marry Beattie, not only would you be the governor here, but a wife can't testify against her husband.
MARTIN	Testify to what?

JEREMY	How about embezzlement? (*Crosses to round table and sits R.*) Our new owner has already shown how inquisitive she can be. When she claps her eyes on those account books of yours, she'll have one or two searching questions to ask you.
MARTIN	To read anything into those account books, you'd have to be a chartered accountant.
JEREMY	(*chuckling*) I've got a sneaking suspicion that's what she is. Anyway, it's about time you thought of settling down. It must be better than doing five years for embezzlement.
MARTIN	You think so?
	(RAHMU *enters from verandah.*)
RAHMU	Excuse me, Sahib.
	(JEREMY *and* MARTIN *turn, startled.*)
MARTIN	How long have you been out there?
RAHMU	Only a moment, Sahib. I fear the rains have started.
JEREMY	You don't know what's happened, do you?
RAHMU	No, Sahib.
	(BEATRICE *enters carrying scarf.*)
BEATRICE	(*to brothers*) Would you two boys mind going upstairs and giving Miss Lupitya a hand?
MARTIN	Isn't Landau up there?
BEATRICE	Yes, but he's not much good. He took one butchers at the body and then we had to stick his head between his knees.
JEREMY	OK Beattie. (*He exits.*)
MARTIN	Don't do anything until I come down. (*He exits.*)
RAHMU	What is it, what has happened?

BEATRICE	Prepare yourself for a little bit of a shock, Rahmu. My poor sister's been murdered. (*Holding scarf out.*) I found this scarf round her neck.
	(RAHMU *takes scarf and sinks to knees with a horrifying wail.*)
	Oh, my Gawd!
RAHMU	Vishnu! Siva! Brama!
BEATRICE	On, don't take on so.
RAHMU	Brama! Brama!
BEATRICE	Well, hang on, I'll see if we got any.
	(*She looks through the bottles of alcohol.*)
RAHMU	She was greatest, kindest lady in the world.
BEATRICE	There's no Brama, dear. (*She offers him a handkerchief.*)
RAHMU	It is not possible. How can Krishna be so cruel.
BEATRICE	There, there. I know its tragic but you mustn't take on so.
	(RAHMU *wails again.*)
	You got to remember, she was a very, very old lady. It's not as if she'd had her prime cut off. She'd had a marvellous innings.
RAHMU	And now she has gone to her death.
BEATRICE	Oh, well, that's life.
RAHMU	I want to die also.
BEATRICE	Now that's enough of that sort of talk. It's no use us all going to pieces. And always remember, it's darkest before dawn.
	(RAHMU *begins to rise but there is a tremendous clap of thunder and he falls to his knees again.*)
RAHMU	My god is angry.
BEATRICE	Is he?

RAHMU	It does not bode well for the killer of my mistress.
BEATRICE	Well, I'm very glad to hear that.
RAHMU	(*rising*) She shall have a funeral fit for a queen.
BEATRICE	Of course she will.
RAHMU	She shall float down the Ganges on a burning pyre.
BEATRICE	Well, that sounds a bit ostentatious to me — but we'll see what her insurance will run to. I say, Rahm; I haven't got a thing to wear for the funeral. When will it be?
RAHMU	Tomorrow.
BEATRICE	As soon as that?
RAHMU	Of course.
BEATRICE	Oh, yes. I forgot. I suppose you daren't keep them hanging about too long in this heat. Trouble is, you don't pack for a funeral. I mean it's not the sort of thing that occurs to you. I only found her two days ago. I didn't expect to lose her so soon.

(RAHMU *starts to moan.*)

Oh, don't start that again, take a grip on yourself.

(LANDAU *enters.*)

How are you feeling now, Mr Landau? |
LANDAU	Rahmu, get me a drink will you.
RAHMU	Yes, Sahib. Whisky, Gin . . .
LANDAU	Anything.
BEATRICE	Make it a brandy and make it two.
RAHMU	No, Memsahib — it is against my religion.
BEATRICE	No, not for you, you daft bat, for me.

(RAHMU *picks up tray and crosses to drinks.*) |

LANDAU	I had a presentiment of disaster as soon as I entered this house.
BEATRICE	You'd get on well with Edie Chalk.
LANDAU	Who?
BEATRICE	Edie Chalk. My friend in Halifax.
LANDAU	Oh, her. Yes.
BEATRICE	She gets funny feelings all the time, does Edie.
LANDAU	Dreadful business, dreadful.
BEATRICE	Awful, I grant you.
LANDAU	I should never have come.
BEATRICE	What about me?
LANDAU	Mmm?
BEATRICE	You've only come up the road. I've travelled eighteen thousand miles and I haven't been here five minutes before I find my poor sister stiff as a poker with her eyeballs rolled up.
LANDAU	Yes, yes, quite.
RAHMU	Your brandy, Memsahib.
BEATRICE	Ta.
RAHMU	Sahib.
LANDAU	Thank you. (*He takes drink and has a sip.*)
BEATRICE	I'll never forget those eyes. They were like poached eggs.
LANDAU	(*hastily puts his drink down*) Mrs Horrocks, please.
BEATRICE	Oh sorry love, still feeling queasy, are you?
LANDAU	Has anyone been onto the police yet?
BEATRICE	Don't think so. There hasn't been time.
LANDAU	(*goes to the phone*) Well, there's absolutely nothing we can do until they arrive. Rahmu, see that none of the houseboys leave the premises.

BEATRICE	(*pointing to phone*) You're wasting your time with that thing, aren't you?
LANDAU	I'd forgotten. (*Tapping.*) Well, there's always a chance it was only temporary.
BEATRICE	Here, wait a minute. (*She goes onto verandah and traces telephone wire.*)
LANDAU	(*putting down phone*) Go on, Rahmu. Tell the staff to remain in their quarters.
RAHMU	If Sahib will permit me to say —
LANDAU	(*on edge*) Just do as you're told.
RAHMU	(*looking hard at* LANDAU) This crime could not have been committed by a Hindu.
LANDAU	I am not interested in your theories Rahmu, I —
RAHMU	The killer is someone staying in this house.
	(BEATRICE *is now at the top of the steps holding telephone lead.*)
BEATRICE	I say, we've been cut off all right.
LANDAU	(*amazed*) That's been severed.
BEATRICE	You don't say.
LANDAU	I mean on purpose. With a sharp instrument.
BEATRICE	With scissors.
LANDAU	Or a knife, one can't be sure.
BEATRICE	With scissors. Been a knife it would only be squashed in on one side. But if you look at this, you can see it's been squeezed in on the both. Scissors.
LANDAU	(*puzzled, looks at it and then at her*) Are you some sort of detective?
BEATRICE	No, a draper. And there's not much I don't know about scissors.
RAHMU	Memsahib is very observant.

LANDAU	Who'd want to do a thing like that?
BEATRICE	Same person as want to do a thing like that. (*She points up.*)
LANDAU	Rahmu, we must get hold of the police in Janakpur. (*To* RAHMU.) Where's the nearest telephone?
RAHMU	In Janakpur.
LANDAU	Damn.
BEATRICE	Well, hang on. Where's the nearest neighbour?
RAHMU	Beyond Janakpur.
BEATRICE	Well then, one of us must drive into the village right away. Do you have a vehicle of some kind?
RAHMU	Yes, Sahib. Martin Sahib has Land Rover.
LANDAU	Right, I'll take that. Bring it round to the front, will you?
RAHMU	Very good, Sahib. (RAHMU *bows and moves to go.*)
LANDAU	Rahmu. How far is it to Janakpur?
RAHMU	Oh, six miles to the bridge, and then another three. A little over twenty miles. (*Exits.*)
LANDAU	With any luck I should be back within the hour.
BEATRICE	Bit quick off the mark, aren't you?
LANDAU	My dear good woman, someone has to go.
BEATRICE	But why you? Why not one of the servants?
LANDAU	Because they are totally unreliable. Once they'd get clear, they might never come back.
BEATRICE	Same applies to you, doesn't it?

LANDAU	You're being ridiculous. How on earth could I be involved in such a hideous affair? I'd never met Lady Eppingham until yesterday.
BEATRICE	That's what you say.
LANDAU	But I don't stand to gain anything whatsoever. I'm a disinterested party, and I ask you, do I look like a murderer?
BEATRICE	Did Jack the Ripper?
LANDAU	(*with self control*) Mrs Horrocks, if we are to follow your train of thought to its logical conclusion, then anyone in this house is a potential suspect.
BEATRICE	Ten out of ten.
LANDAU	But on the face of it there is only one person who has actually gained anything from Lady Eppingham's death.
BEATRICE	Who's that?
LANDAU	Yourself.
BEATRICE	On, what a rotten thing to say. Do I look like a murderer?
LANDAU	Did Jack the Ripper?
BEATRICE	So, according to you, short of a carrier pigeon we're all going to be stuck here forever, is that it?
LANDAU	There's any number of us who could go.
BEATRICE	Who?
LANDAU	Well, either of your nephews.
	(VANA *enters.*)
BEATRICE	(*to* LANDAU) Or Miss Lupitya.
LANDAU	(*not seeing her*) No, I think not.
VANA	I beg your pardon?

LANDAU	(*rising*) Oh, I'm sorry. I didn't realise you were there.
VANA	Have you recovered, Mr Landau?
LANDAU	(*on his dignity*) It was only a momentary thing. The heat.
BEATRICE	And them staring eyeballs didn't help none either.
	(LANDAU *gives her an irritated look and takes another sip of his drink.*)
VANA	Have you been able to contact the police yet?
BEATRICE	Not so far.
VANA	But it's imperative. They must come at once.
LANDAU	Exactly what I keep trying to tell Mrs Horrocks.
BEATRICE	Well I'm not arguing with you about it. It's just a question of deciding who's the best person to go.
VANA	Does it matter? (*She sits.*)
BEATRICE	Course it does. I mean, we don't want to send him what done it, do we?
LANDAU	Or *her*.
BEATRICE	You're right anti-women aren't you? I'll lay you six to four he's not married.
	(RAHMU *enters with umbrella.*)
RAHMU	I have brought the car round to the front. But please drive carefully, Sahib. The rain will have washed the surface away.
LANDAU	(*taking umbrella and starts to exit*) Thank you. I'll be as quick as I can.
BEATRICE	Here — hold your horses Mr Landau.
LANDAU	Now look here Mrs Horrocks —

BEATRICE	Belt up!
LANDAU	What?
BEATRICE	Shut your mouth and give your ears a chance.
LANDAU	I've never been spoken to like that in all my life.
BEATRICE	(*to* VANA) I told you he wasn't married. Now, if I'm in charge here, which I am, you'll do as you're told, which you will. If you insist on going, you're not going by yourself.
LANDAU	You'll accompany me, will you?
BEATRICE	No. I'm stopping here to keep an eye on things. You'll go with him. (*Points to* RAHMU) All right with you, Rahmu?
	(*There is a clap of thunder.* RAHMU *and* LANDAU *look at one another.*)
RAHMU	Very good, Memsahib.
LANDAU	I — er — I suppose it's really my duty to stay here.
RAHMU	I shall go alone. (*He bows.*)
LANDAU	(*hurriedly*) No.
RAHMU	Why should I not go by myself?
LANDAU	Because I consider it unwise.
RAHMU	Sahib does not want the police here.
LANDAU	How dare you.
BEATRICE	(*rising and slaps* RAHMU's *hand*) Oy! You ought to be ashamed of yourselves. Carrying on like that with poor Hester still lukewarm. (LANDAU *closes his eyes on the thought of it.*) Now, listen. Anyone object if Miss Lupitya goes with Rahmu? (LANDAU *starts to speak.*) And it's all the same if you do. (*To* VANA.) You don't mind going, do you, dear?

VANA	No. If it is your wish.
BEATRICE	Nice to get a bit of collaboration.
RAHMU	This way, Miss Lupitya.
	(RAHMU *goes.* VANA *start to exit.*)
BEATRICE	And when you get there, don't forget to tell them everything you know.
VANA	Of course — everything. (*She exits.*)
LANDAU	Damn telephone. It makes everything twice as difficult.
BEATRICE	I suppose that was the idea.
LANDAU	No concern of mine of course, but there's the post mortem to arrange, the funeral —
BEATRICE	Post mortem?
LANDAU	Certainly.
BEATRICE	But that'll delay the funeral.
LANDAU	This is murder, Mrs Horrocks.
BEATRICE	But they're going to float here down the Ganges on a burning tyre.

(LANDAU *sighs in exasperation, crosses to desk and sits down.*)

I suppose it's all right. Wouldn't fancy it myself. Bit undignified, if you know what I mean. Here, you know I was telling Rahm that I didn't have anything to wear at the funeral, but don't you think it would be a fitting tribute to my poor sister's memory if I wore her hat? (*She picks up hatbox.*) I mean it fits the bill, doesn't it? Something borrowed, something blue. I'm not averse to a bit of ritual you know. (*She opens hatbox and takes out hat.*) Oh, I say. I rather go for this hat. (*She puts it on.*) How does it look? (*She turns to face* LANDAU. *For the first time we see that the spider is on the brim of the hat.*)

LANDAU	Hmmm?
BEATRICE	(*oblivious to the spider*) Does it look all right?
	(LANDAU *turns to face her. He freezes then gets up in horror. Thunder is heard.*)
	What's the matter? Your tummy playing you up again? Here, you have gone a shocking colour. Shall I get you ... (*She takes a step forward.*)
LANDAU	No! Don't move. Don't move. Don't do anything sudden at all. (*Picks up statue from desk.*) Now, I'm going to have to do something you may find a bit unusual, but whatever happens don't move and don't cry out.
BEATRICE	(*backing away*) Oh my gawd!
LANDAU	Shh. (*He advances.*) Now stay quite still.
BEATRICE	It was you what done it. You're round the bend.
LANDAU	(*picking up an ornament*) Oh no. This is no good. (*Replaces ornament on desk and picks up umbrella from cabinet.*)
	(BEATRICE *backs away.*)
	Stay right where you are. (*He advances.*) Now I shan't hurt you more than is absolutely necessary.
BEATRICE	Why pick on me?
LANDAU	It's not you. It's your hat.
BEATRICE	Well, let me take it off then. (*She reaches up to take it off.*)
LANDAU	No! Put your hands down. (*He advances.*) Now Mrs Horrocks, I shall only be able to hit you once.
	(BEATRICE *faints behind sofa and* LANDAU *lays into her hat with the umbrella. Loud crashes of thunder.* MARTIN *and* JEREMY *enter, and drag* LANDAU *away as he shouts.*)

Dead, dead, dead.

MARTIN   What the hell's going on?

(BEATRICE'S *hand appears grasping the top of the sofa.*)

BEATRICE   Don't let go of him. (MARTIN *crosses to her and helps her up.*) He's round the twist. He's got a thing about hats.

LANDAU   (*pointing to behind sofa*) It was a spider.

BEATRICE   A spider?

MARTIN   Where?

LANDAU   It's dead now. It was on your hat.

(JEREMY *crosses behind sofa and finds mangled spider.*)

BEATRICE   Is that all?

LANDAU   The most dreadful thing I've ever had to face in all my life.

BEATRICE   You ought to be ashamed of yourself. They bring you luck. Me and George used to have a lovely little money spider once. (JEREMY *holds spider over* BEATRICE'S *shoulder.*) It used to dangle over the dressing table and we got very attached to it. (*She sees spider.*) I remember once when he was combing his hair — (*She double-takes and faints on the sofa.*)

MARTIN   Get that damn thing out of here.

JEREMY   Yes sir, very good, sir. (*Crosses to verandah and throws it away.*)

LANDAU   I think she ought to have a brandy.

MARTIN   With or without soda? (*Crosses to drinks.*)

BEATRICE   (*eyes still closed*) Without.

LANDAU   How are you feeling now, Mrs Horrocks?

BEATRICE   Oh, Mr Landau, do you forgive me, but the way you were looking at me. I thought I was a gonner —

LANDAU	Yes, yes. I daresay.
BEATRICE	Now, of course, I can see how very brave you were.
LANDAU	(*pleased*) Well, er — one does have to rise to these things when the occasion demands.
MARTIN	(*handing her drink*) Here, knock this back.
BEATRICE	(*taking it*) Oh, I don't usually start this early, but we'll call it medicinal. (*She knocks it back in one gulp.*) Ta. I'll have the other half.
	(MARTIN *takes her glass and refills it.*)
BEATRICE	Here, I suppose in time you get used to all these creepy-crawlies out here?
LANDAU	I can't honestly say that I have.
JEREMY	No, nor Martin.
BEATRICE	Oh, dear. (*To* LANDAU.) I say, Mr Landau, there hasn't been a mistake, has there? I mean my sister did definitely want me to have this place?
LANDAU	No doubt whatsoever.
BEATRICE	Oh, I see. Well, I'll just have to get busy with the Flit Gun then. (MARTIN, *with drink, taps her shoulder.*) Ooooh! (*She jumps.*) I thought it was the merry widow. (*Takes drink.*) Not that I won't be able to cope. Matter of fact, I was going to go through those ledgers this afternoon. I suppose you do use double-entry book-keeping?
MARTIN	Well, they're in a hell of a mess at the moment. I'll tell you what, let me have them for a couple of days, and I'll get them into some sort of order —
BEATRICE	Oh, don't trouble yourself. I'll be able to follow them all right.
JEREMY	(*to* MARTIN) I think some statements should be taken from the staff before the police get here.

MARTIN	Good idea. (*He starts to go.*)
JEREMY	No, no, no. (*Pointedly.*) Mr Landau and I can see to that, can't we Mr Landau?
LANDAU	Will Mrs Horrocks be all right with your brother?
MARTIN	Why shouldn't she be?
JEREMY	Oh yes. Plenty of girls around here would give a lot for that.
BEATRICE	Oh, I see. He's a bit of a lady killer, is he?
JEREMY	Yes.
BEATRICE	I say, Martin, I hope you didn't take my last remark too literal, dear. About you being a lady killer, I mean.
MARTIN	Of course not, Beattie. (*Rises*) This sort of thing is bound to make us all feel a bit edgy. (*Goes to take her glass.*)
BEATRICE	Oh, I don't think I'd better have another. I'll be tiddly poohs.
MARTIN	(*takes her glass and crosses to drinks*) Please yourself. I'm going to have one.
BEATRICE	All right then. I expect you're feeling the strain a bit too, eh?
MARTIN	Not particularly.
BEATRICE	(*picking up crushed hat*) I don't think I can wear this no more. I shall just have to hold it as the dog said when he was half-way across the Sahara. (*She laughs uproariously.*)
MARTIN	(*crosses to* BEATRICE *with drinks*) You know, Beattie, there's more to you than meets the eye.
BEATRICE	Well, as my George used to say, 'Once round you Beattie, twice round the gas works.'
MARTIN	Nonsense, you're fine. (*Hands her drink.*)

BEATRICE	No, I mean, let's face it. I do rather tend to run to fat. Well, I say run, it's more a headlong dash really.
MARTIN	You don't do yourself justice. I wouldn't give you twopence for a skinny woman.
BEATRICE	They're all the go now. Topless, bottomless and hopeless.
MARTIN	Not *my* type, I assure you.
BEATRICE	Oh, go on!
MARTIN	No. When I settle down it will be with a mature woman.
BEATRICE	Oh well, now we know your specifications, we'll have to find you a nice little wife.
MARTIN	As a matter of fact, I think I've already found one.
BEATRICE	Oh Martin, isn't that nice. Have you known her long?
MARTIN	Not very.
BEATRICE	That's the best way to start a marriage. I often think you can know too much about each other. No point in starting off knowing you've made a mistake. Let it creep up on you gradually.
MARTIN	That's a point.
BEATRICE	Have you and your young lady named the day yet?
MARTIN	To tell you the truth I haven't had the courage to ask her to marry me yet.
BEATRICE	Oh, Martin. You are silly. Somebody else might come and fall under her spell.
MARTIN	I don't think that's very likely. (*He moves to behind her.*)
BEATRICE	Oh, I see. What's she like then? Back of a bus?

MARTIN	Good God, no. More — em —
BEATRICE	More homely?
MARTIN	That's the word.
BEATRICE	Well anyway, Martin, you don't want to let the grass grow under your feet. You want to take your courage in both hands and say, 'Beloved, will you marry me?'
MARTIN	You're right, of course. Beloved will you marry me?
BEATRICE	That's it, but with a bit more feeling.
MARTIN	Will you marry me?
BEATRICE	That's better.
MARTIN	Well, will you?
BEATRICE	(*blankly*) Eh?
MARTIN	Marry me.
BEATRICE	(*flabbergasted*) What?
MARTIN	What's your answer, Beattie?
BEATRICE	I'll have another brandy.
MARTIN	I'm quite serious, Beattie.
BEATRICE	What me? At my age?
MARTIN	I told you I preferred my women matured.
BEATRICE	Matured yes, but not vintage.
MARTIN	(*kneels*) Don't refuse me, Beattie. My life out here has been a nightmare and I can't deny it's left its mark on me. But I believe providence has brought us together and I'll make you a good husband. I swear it. What do you say?
BEATRICE	Pull the other one, it's got bells on it.
MARTIN	I don't think you understand.
BEATRICE	I understand alright. What are you up to?
MARTIN	What do you mean?

BEATRICE	I might not have had a posh education, but I know a wrong 'un when I see one.
MARTIN	(*changing his tune*) Then go back to where you came from, you damned interfering old busybody!
BEATRICE	(*rising to him*) Ah, now that's more like our charming Martin.
MARTIN	Don't say I didn't warn you. If you don't get out of here while you've got the chance, you're going to end up as dead as your sister.
BEATRICE	We'll see about that!

(*She opens the door and in comes* RAHMU *carrying* VANA *in his arms.*)

CURTAIN

Beatrice and Martin argue

Lady Hester and Landau

Scene Three

*The same, that evening. The rain has stopped for a
moment, and most of the thunder heard during the
scene is in the distance. The blinds are down along
the verandah and the curtain is drawn across the
door D.L. BEATRICE, MARTIN and JEREMY are
sitting round the room, eyeing each other. LANDAU
is pacing up and down. Nobody speaks. The
record player is playing some Indian music. After a
pause there is a knock on the door.*

BEATRICE   (*jumping*) Who is it?

(RAHMU *enters pushing the trolley on which there
is an assortment of curry dishes. The* HOUSEBOY
follows him in and helps to serve.)

RAHMU   Dinner is ready, Memsahib.

BEATRICE   Good.

RAHMU   It is most unusual to serve dinner in the
drawing-room.

BEATRICE   I've asked you to serve it in here so as we
can all keep an eye on each other. Less
people we have wandering around on their
own the better. Go on, bung it round, dear.
(*She gets up and collects cutlery.*)

JEREMY   Smells good. Is it the Madras?

RAHMU   No, Sahib, the vindaloo.

JEREMY   Will that be all right for Mrs Horrocks?

BEATRICE   (*handing him cutlery*) Eh? What?

RAHMU   You're eating vindaloo.

BEATRICE   (*puzzled*) In the where?

RAHMU   Very hot Indian curry.

BEATRICE   Oh, lovely.

(JEREMY *moves table to R. of sofa and sits down.*
LANDAU *sits.*)

MARTIN   Get her something milder.

BEATRICE | I can eat curry with the best of them. He's the one that needs cooling off. (*Handing* MARTIN *his cutlery.*) Here's your chopsticks. We've got stacks of Indian restaurants in Halifax. There's more *Stars of India* in the Cleckheaton Road than you've had hot dinners.

(VANA *enters. She has a bandaged wrist.* MARTIN *rises.*)

Oh, Miss Lupitya. How are you feeling?

VANA | A little better, thank you. Fortunately, I have a very thick head.

MARTIN | And a very pretty one. (*Helps her into chair.*) You shouldn't have come down so soon.

BEATRICE | (*to* VANA) You want to watch him, love. He's on the rebound.

MARTIN | You're lucky to be alive at all, Miss Lupitya.

BEATRICE | She is, in this house.

(*Thunder is heard.*)

LANDAU | I don't find that very amusing, Mrs Horrocks.

BEATRICE | Neither do I.

LANDAU | (*rising*) How the hell are we —

BEATRICE | Language, Basil.

LANDAU | How the blazes —

BEATRICE | That's better.

LANDAU | — are we going to get the police here now the confounded bridge is down.

JEREMY | (*casually*) We'll just have to wait until it's put up again.

RAHMU | (*handing curry to* VANA) Miss Lupitya.

VANA | Rahmu, I haven't had a chance to thank you for avoiding a more serious accident.

LANDAU	He drove you straight into a tree. What precisely did he avoid?
BEATRICE	A two hundred foot chasm.
LANDAU	We only have his word for that.
RAHMU	(*angrily*) I tell you the bridge is broken.
BEATRICE	All right, keep your turban on. (*To* LANDAU.) And you stop upsetting the servants.
VANA	I can assure you the reason we swerved off the road was to avoid certain death.
JEREMY	Whenever the rains come that bridge is the first thing to go.
LANDAU	(*referring to record*) I wish you'd turn that infernal thing off.
BEATRICE	Oh, I rather like it.
LANDAU	Well, I don't.
BEATRICE	Oh, isn't he an Auntie Mary? Go on then Jeremy, turn it off.
	(*He does so.*)
JEREMY	All right, Beattie.
LANDAU	Thank you.
BEATRICE	God help your wife, if ever you get one.
LANDAU	I doubt if *any* of us will get *anything* ever again.
RAHMU	(*handing him curry*) Your curry, Sahib.
BEATRICE	You was wrong, wasn't you?
VANA	Is the telephone still out of order?
LANDAU	It was cut.
VANA	(*puzzled*) Cut?
BEATRICE	With scissors.
RAHMU	(*handing curry to* MARTIN) Master Martin.
BEATRICE	I found that out. No one else spotted that but me. And I tell you, you find them scissors and you've found the murderer.

LANDAU	Yes, yes, yes. The point is, without the police being here, nothing can be solved.
RAHMU	(*handing curry to* JEREMY) Master Jeremy.
BEATRICE	Here, not so much of the 'masters'. What about your mistress? (*She laughs.*) That would have pulverised my George. (*She realises that no one else is laughing.*) What's the matter with you all?
LANDAU	You'll forgive us if we can't share your levity.
BEATRICE	Well, you've got to put a brave face on a situation like this. I mean, like they say, 'eat, drink and be merry for tomorrow we...' (*Changes the subject.*) Got my grub there, Rahmu?
RAHMU	(*handing her curry*) Yes, Memsahib, but only a little to start with.
BEATRICE	Don't keep on. I tell you I'm used to this spicy stuff. Horseradish sauce, ketchup. I'm a devil for roll top herrings. (*She takes spoonful and savours it.*) It's not hot at all. I'll tell you what it tastes like. Lancashire hot pot with a dollop of Marmite. (*The curry hits her.*) Oh my gawd! (*She leaps up.*)
LANDAU	Has something struck you?
BEATRICE	Not 'arf. (*She points to her ears.*) Can't you see the smoke coming out of my ears?
VANA	I think Mrs Horrocks would like a glass of water.
BEATRICE	Never mind about the glass. Give us the jug! (*She drinks from water jug.*)
	(RAHMU *slaps* HOUSEBOY *who is laughing.* HOUSEBOY *goes out*)
	Oh, what are you playing at, Rahmu? Are you trying to poison me?
RAHMU	No, Memsahib.

BEATRICE	(*sitting*) Because if that's your idea of a joke, you can collect your cards.
LANDAU	We've all had the same, Mrs Horrocks.
BEATRICE	I think I've burnt my uvula.
LANDAU	Have a banana.
BEATRICE	Same to you.
VANA	No. It does help to cool the mouth.
BEATRICE	Oh. Peel us one of them will you, Rahm?
RAHMU	Yes, Memsahib.
MARTIN	You ought to have stayed at home.
BEATRICE	I am at home.
	(*Thunder is heard.*)
MARTIN	Your other one. The sooner you get back to chip butties, the better.
BEATRICE	(*rounding on him*) Oh yes, you'd love that, wouldn't you. You'd like to keep me quiet one way or another.
	(RAHMU *hands her a banana.*)
	Ta.
MARTIN	Stupid woman.
BEATRICE	Oh, so I'm stupid now, am I? (*Turns to* LANDAU.) This morning he wanted to marry me. Can you imagine that?
LANDAU	Good God no!
BEATRICE	No. Neither can I. And when that little ruse failed, he tried to doctor my curry.
MARTIN	Oh really!
LANDAU	That's a dangerous accusation!
BEATRICE	Oh, is it? Well, let me tell you that curry isn't the only thing he's been doctoring. Boy, you ought to see them accounts. A Harley Street surgeon couldn't have carved

	them up better. (*Evryone stops and looks at her.*) Yes, I've been doing a bit of homework this afternoon. You just ask him how they pick four hundred ton of tea a year and only two hundred go through the books.
MARTIN	That is a damn lie.
VANA	Be careful, Mrs Horrocks.
BEATRICE	No. He's one that ought to be careful.
JEREMY	Just a minute, Beattie. Are you absolutely sure of your facts?
BEATRICE	Positive. Big brother's on the fiddle.
JEREMY	Martin, I'm surprised at you.
MARTIN	What the hell are you talking about?
JEREMY	It's all right. I'm sure Beattie won't prefer charges. Now, where are they then, these ledgers?
BEATRICE	Never you mind.
JEREMY	Oh, come now Beattie. If you're going to accuse poor old Martin in front of witnesses, you ought to produce the proof.
BEATRICE	I'll do that when the police get here and not before. I don't think I trust anyone in this house. (*They protest.*) No, Not anyone.
	(*Thunder is heard.*)
JEREMY	How about that, Landau? Not even the law is above suspicion in this house.
LANDAU	As I've already pointed out, there is only one person who could gain from Lady Eppingham's death, and that's Mrs Horrocks.
JEREMY	Ah! A Daniel come to judgment.
LANDAU	One doesn't have to be a lawyer to work that out.
BEATRICE	And how do we know you are?

LANDAU	Hmm? Are what?
BEATRICE	Well, you keep saying you're a solicitor, how do I know you're certified?
LANDAU	Oh, really!
BEATRICE	Things aren't always what they seem, you know. A cat can have kittens in the oven, but that doesn't make them biscuits.
VANA	Mrs Horrocks, I can vouch for the fact that he is my senior partner.
BEATRICE	Oh? And who's going to vouch for you then, him?
LANDAU	Certainly.
BEATRICE	I see. She scratches your back, you scratch hers.
RAHMU	There is only one person who can tell you who murdered Lady Eppingham.
BEATRICE	Who?
RAHMU	Lady Eppingham. (*He exits.*)
LANDAU	Superstitious people.
MARTIN	Poor old Rahmu. He spends as much time in the next world as he does in this.
VANA	Each to his own belief, Mr Eppingham.
BEATRICE	It's worth a try though.
LANDAU	What is?
BEATRICE	Calling up the dead.
LANDAU	Calling up the what?
BEATRICE	You know, table tapping.
LANDAU	Rubbish!
JEREMY	(*rubbing his hands*) No. Great come on. Clear the table.
LANDAU	Mumbo-jumbo.
JEREMY	Oh, be a sport.

BEATRICE	Can't do any harm to ask her.
MARTIN	Ask her what?
BEATRICE	Who snuffed her out.
LANDAU	Well, I refuse to take part.
BEATRICE	Why? You frightened your name will come floating down the chimney?
JEREMY	Well, I'm game. How about you, Miss Lupitya?
VANA	(*pause*) Yes.
JEREMY	Great.
BEATRICE	Now hands up all those in favour of calling up my sister?
	(BEATRICE, JEREMY *and* VANA *raise their hands.* LANDAU *and* MARTIN *abstain.*)
	Oh, hard luck, you're outvoted three to two.
JEREMY	Come on then, draw up your chairs.
LANDAU	Well, if I must — I suppose I must.
BEATRICE	Right. Now, what do we do?
JEREMY	Don't you know?
BEATRICE	Not really, no.
LANDAU	I said it was rubbish.
JEREMY	How about you, Miss Lupitya? Do you know the drill?
VANA	I have never practised it, no.
BEATRICE	Well, it can't be all that difficult. I mean Edie Chalk only went a couple of times and she's not that quick on the uptake. She was the one who tried to talk me into getting in touch with my George after he'd went.
JEREMY	Why didn't you?
BEATRICE	We weren't on speaking terms. Here, I hope it works with this storm about.

JEREMY	Why shouldn't it?
BEATRICE	Well, if Hester's wafting through the atmosphere, she don't want to get caught up on a bit of forked lightning. Now, what are we going to do? Cards, fingertips or the moving glass?
LANDAU	What?
BEATRICE	What method shall we use?
LANDAU	Can't make any difference. You'll never reach her.
BEATRICE	Why not? What time is it? (*Looks at her watch.*) She can't have got far.
JEREMY	Why don't we try the glass, first.
BEATRICE	Yes. From what I hear about the way she could soak it up, she ought to come through a brandy glass a treat.
JEREMY	Right. Then here we are, Beattie. (*He hands her a glass.*)
LANDAU	Assuming Lady Eppingham is prepared to visit us, how precisely is she going to utilise the glass?
BEATRICE	Well, once she's got inside, she shoots round the table giving us little messages. Least, that's what Edie Chalk says. She does it every Christmas now round her place. Not that I've been, but by all accounts it's very gay. After supper, they have a bit of a knees up, and then call up the dead. It's ever so jolly.
MARTIN	I can't wait to meet Edie.
BEATRICE	Yes, you'd get on well with her. She's looking for a husband. Oh, silly old me. I'm forgetting the most important part. I'm forgetting the bits of paper.
LANDAU	Paper?

BEATRICE	Yes. All round the table you've got to have letters like, A, B, C, D, E, F, G, H, I, J, K, L, M, N, O, P...
LANDAU	(*long suffering*) The alphabet.
BEATRICE	Yes. How many bits shall we need?
LANDAU	I should try twenty-six.
BEATRICE	Oh, and apart from that, we've got to have two extra pieces of paper.
LANDAU	What are they for?
BEATRICE	They've got 'yes' and 'no' written on them, and I'll tell you for why. Edie Chalk once explained it to me. She said these spirits get right fed up pushing this glass about, going Y — E — S and N — O —
JEREMY	Listen, why don't we just stick to 'yes' and 'no'. It'll make it much easier for Aunt Hester.
BEATRICE	What a good idea. I say, Martin, it's going to be exciting, isn't it? Right, now who's got a pair of scissors.
VANA	I have.
	(BEATRICE *slowly looks up at her.*)
BEATRICE	(*quietly*) Oh, have you?
	(*Everyone now looks at* VANA, *who then realises what she has said.*)
VANA	(*hesitantly*) I always carry nail scissors with me. Most women do.
BEATRICE	I don't. (*To* LANDAU.) Do you?
	(LANDAU *reacts to this.*)
VANA	(*looking through her bag*) I'm sure there must be more than one pair of scissors in the house. (*She looks up.*) That's strange.
MARTIN	What?
VANA	They seem to be missing.

BEATRICE	(*offering to take the bag*) Let's have a look.
LANDAU	When did you last have them?
VANA	I can't be sure.
BEATRICE	Well, they're not here now.
	(*Thunder is heard.*)
JEREMY	The sooner we get in touch with Aunt Hester, the better.
BEATRICE	We'll just have to tear the paper then. Come on, Martin, take a pew.
MARTIN	Might as well be hung for a sheep.
JEREMY	(*laughing*) What's the next step, teacher?
BEATRICE	Cheeky. Well, after we've invited Hester to step inside, we all put our fingers lightly on the glass, and consecrate like hell.
JEREMY	Here we are then, 'yes' and 'no'. (*Places 'yes' and 'no' at either end of the table.*)
BEATRICE	(*points to pieces of paper*) And for goodness sake, don't nobody sneeze.
VANA	And who will be our spokesman?
BEATRICE	Eh?
MARTIN	Some damn fool's got to ask the questions.
BEATRICE	That'll be me, of course.
LANDAU	Course.
VANA	But have you got extra-sensory perception?
BEATRICE	Certainly not.
VANA	But surely we should find out first if we have a person here with powers?
BEATRICE	All right then. Anybody here feel they're physic?
	(*They all shake their heads.*)
	No? Right. Well, I'll ask the questions, then. Fingers on the glass. Oh, Edie Chalk should really be here you know. She's really

	quite good at this. I'll never forget Derby Day she come into my shop. Beattie, she said, four's your lucky number today. Stick with the fours and you won't go far wrong. Did you know, the Derby was the fourth race?
LANDAU	(*bored*) No, I didn't.
BEATRICE	Well, it was. So I went straight to the till, and took out *four* pounds and put it on the number *four* horse. Well, that's following your luck, isn't it? Four pounds on the fourth horse in the fourth race.
JEREMY	Did it win?
BEATRICE	Come fourth.
MARTIN	Well, as Mrs Chalk isn't with us, let's for God's sake get on with it.
BEATRICE	Don't you talk to me like that. At least I'm trying to do something constructive. And if this seance is going to work, we've got to have complete harmony.
LANDAU	And, presumably, silence.
BEATRICE	Yes. So shut up. Now come on, get your fingers on.

(*They all concentrate. Nothing happens. After a few seconds silence,* LANDAU *clears his throat. Another pause, then* BEATRICE *speaks in a whisper.*)

Hester...can you hear me, Hester? (*To the others.*) You can't expect her to come through all at once. Like the radio. She's got to warm up first. (*Pause.*) Hester...Hester...we need you, we want your help...Hester?

(*There are three knocks at the door. They all freeze.* BEATRICE *speaks in a hoarse whisper.*)

Ooh crumbs! She's arrived. (*A little louder.*) Come in and speak.

(RAHMU *enters*.)

RAHMU	Do you want your tea now?
BEATRICE	We'll have tea in a minute, dear. We're trying to call up my sister.
RAHMU	No, no. You must not do that. I have seen a sign in the sky.
BEATRICE	Stop interfering.
RAHMU	I tell you, I have seen the sign.
BEATRICE	All right, so you've seen it. Now pipe down.
RAHMU	It means death.

(*Thunder is heard.*)

BEATRICE	Don't be so hysterical. We're having a go, so stand over there and be quiet.
JEREMY	(*leading* RAHMU up the steps) Come on, Rahmu.
VANA	I'm sure I'm right in saying the other world can only reach us through a medium.
BEATRICE	Well, we haven't got one, so we'll have to soldier on.

(LANDAU *does not co-operate.* JEREMY *switches one of the lights out.*)

	Who did that?
JEREMY	I did! Aunt Hester never cared for bright lights.
BEATRICE	Oh no, Jeremy. It's spooky. We'll all get the collywobbles.
MARTIN	Look, if we're going to do it, let's get on with it.
BEATRICE	Yes. Fingers on the glass. (*Sees that* LANDAU *hasn't joined in.*) I said fingers on, Mr Landau. Oh, come on, do as you're told. It won't work otherwise.

(LANDAU *still doesn't move.*)

	What's up? You gone deaf or something?
	(*They all stare at* LANDAU.)
	He's dead.
VANA	(*shocked*) Oh, no.
	(*A strange moan comes from* LANDAU*'s lips. For a moment no one realises where the sound is coming from.*)
BEATRICE	(*whispering in fright*) Who's doing that?
	(LANDAU *moans again.*)
JEREMY	It's Landau. Probably the curry.
BEATRICE	Crumbs, we must have sent him off.
	(LANDAU *gives a throttled sound and then speaks in a weird voice.*)
LANDAU	Beattie — Beattie —
BEATRICE	(*excitedly*) Shh! Don't nobody move. We've got through. (*Pause*) Is your name Hester Eppingham?
LANDAU	No. George 'Orrocks.
BEATRICE	(*stunned for a moment, then*) How the bloody hell did you get here?
LANDAU	I'eard you calling.
BEATRICE	Since when has your name been Hester?
LANDAU	Tell me you're all right, Beattie.
BEATRICE	Course I'm all right. Now get off the line.
VANA	We want to speak to Lady Eppingham.
BEATRICE	I'm doing the asking. We want to speak to Lady Eppingham. Hester, can you hear me?
	(*There is a flash of lightning. The lights go out. Thunder is heard.*)
JEREMY	Must have hit the power cables.
RAHMU	I do not like the dark.

MARTIN	The generator. I'll go and switch over to the generator.
BEATRICE	Soon as you've done it you come straight back. And let's have the rest of you stock still. I'm not having the witnesses nobbled.
RAHMU	I saw the sign. It means death for somebody.
BEATRICE	You, if you don't belt up. AAhh!
JEREMY	What's the matter?
VANA	I'm so sorry, Mrs Horrocks. I was looking for my handbag.
BEATRICE	Well, don't do that again. (*The lights come back on.*) Oh, well done, Martin.
	(LANDAU *starts to moan again.*)
	Oh blimey. Here we go again.
LANDAU	(*in a high-pitched voice*) Sister.
BEATRICE	Eh? Is that you, Hester?
LANDAU	Sister.
BEATRICE	Yes, that's alright.
LANDAU	Hear me.
BEATRICE	Speak up dear, you're very faint. I expect her throat's still bothering 'er.
LANDAU	Listen to me — listen.
BEATRICE	We are listening, dear.
LANDAU	I was — murdered.
	(RAHMU *falls to his knees again.*)
RHAMU	Vishnu, Siva Brama —
BEATRICE	Will you shut up?
LANDAU	Murdered —
BEATRICE	Could you see who the murderer was?
LANDAU	He — he —

	(There is a flash of lightning.)
BEATRICE	So it was a man.
LANDAU	Ring — ring —
BEATRICE	You mean like an engagement ring?
LANDAU	Aaaaahhhhhh. *(His voice fades away.)*
VANA	She is going from us.
BEATRICE	Don't go yet, dear, you've only just arrived.
LANDAU	Ah! *(He emits one last terrifying wail, clutches his throat, and his head slumps forward.)*
BEATRICE	*(pause)* That's not curry.
JEREMY	Is he alright?
Vana	Yes, I think so. He has fainted, that is all.
RAHMU	Martin, Sahib!
BEATRICE	Eh?
RAHMU	Martin Sahib wears the ring.
JEREMY	What do you mean?
RAHMU	The ring — the ring — she saw the ring.
JEREMY	Martin's not the only man who wears a ring.
BEATRICE	He is, in this house.
	(RAHMU shows his hands. JEREMY looks down at his own. VANA lifts up LANDAU's hands.)
JEREMY	It couldn't be Martin.
BEATRICE	Well, he hasn't come back, has he?
JEREMY	I tell you it can't be.
RAHMU	He is the killer.
JEREMY	It's a lie. It's a lie. We were going to do it with the spider — *(The others stare at him.)* — but we never got the chance. That's the truth. It must be. Martin, Martin. *(JEREMY rushes out through the verandah.)*

VANA	We must follow them, Rahmu. Make sure they don't do anything foolish. (*Thunder is heard;* VANA *rushes out after* JEREMY.)
RAHMU	I will call the houseboys. (*Exits U.C.*)
	(LANDAU *starts to wail again.*)
BEATRICE	He's coming up for the third time.
LANDAU	Beattie — Beattie —
BEATRICE	It's all right, love. We've got him. It's all over.
LANDAU	Ring — ring —
BEATRICE	Yes, we know, dear — Martin's ring.
LANDAU	No. Ring — bell — bell — ring —
BEATRICE	Bell, bell ring?
LANDAU	Ring bell for Rahmu —
BEATRICE	What, now?
LANDAU	No — I was in — my room — I — ring for Rahmu —
BEATRICE	Yes.
LANDAU	I had been looking for Will. Found letter —
BEATRICE	Letter? Who from?
LANDAU	Rahmu's sister — she and Harry — it was Rahmu. Rahmu killed me.
	(LANDAU *emits an almighty wail and again sinks back into the chair.*)
BEATRICE	Mr Landau — darling — Bas! (*She starts to run to door D.L.*) Jeremy — Jeremy. (*As she gets to the door,* RAHMU *flings open the curtains. There is a clap of thunder. His eyes are blazing.*)
RAHMU	Memsahib.
BEATRICE	Rahmu, why did you kill poor Hester?
RAHMU	She found out that I killed her husband.
BEATRICE	You mean it was you that shot Sir Harry?

RAHMU

Yes. Because the native girl he shamed was my sister. Sir Harry's death unbalanced Memsahib's mind and I was able to persuade her that she was responsible for his murder.

BEATRICE

Oh, what a dreadful thing to do.

RAHMU

And my mistress was always most grateful that I never betrayed her secret. And you, Memsahib, will not betray mine.

(RAHMU gets the scarf round BEATRICE's neck and they start to struggle behind the sofa.)

BEATRICE

(choking) No. Course I won't Mr Landau, wake up. I'm the soul of discretion. You ask Edie Chalk.

(There is a flash of lightning. The lights flicker. LANDAU stirs as BEATRICE and RAHMU fall behind the sofa. He wakes up and sees them fighting. He picks up the brass table top and strikes RAHMU's head behind the sofa. A 'gong' sound is heard followed by thunder.)

LANDAU

(to BEATRICE) Are you all right?

BEATRICE

(appearing from behind sofa) I'll say one thing, you're not just a pretty face, are you?

LANDAU

Is he dead?

BEATRICE

No. But he's doing a lot of heavy breathing.

LANDAU

I don't feel too good myself.

BEATRICE

I'm not surprised, the trance you was in. Anyway, you'll feel better after a good night's sleep. First thing tomorrow, I want you to draw up them contracts.

LANDAU

Contracts?

BEATRICE

For them poor pluckers. I'm going to put this place back on its feet. It won't be easy, but I'll do it.

LANDAU	You know, I think perhaps you will, Beattie.
BEATRICE	I will, if I can get some people round me that I can trust. What about you coming in on the management, Bas? (*She sits on his lap.*)
LANDAU	Management?
BEATRICE	Yes, why not? You've got the qualifications. Miss Lupitya was telling me you got B.F. at Oxford.
LANDAU	(*smiles*) Very kind of you, Beattie. Most tempting, but I don't know if my firm will approve.
BEATRICE	They don't have to know anything about it.
LANDAU	Well, perhaps there'd be no harm in my becoming a sleeping partner.
BEATRICE	(*naughtily*) Wahay!!

CURTAIN

PROPERTY LIST

Act ONE

On Stage	Bottles of drinks & glasses on drinks cupboard
	Records
	Papers in desk drawer
	Hand-bell on table
	Gramophone
Off Stage	Briefcase containing legal papers (Landau)
	Hat & spectacles (Landau)
	Fan (Auntie)
	Suitcase & briefcase with codicil (Vana)

Act ONE, Scene 2

On Stage	Two tin baths on verandah
	Ladder
	Duster (Beatrice)
	Rubber gloves on verandah chair
	Ivory elephant on table
	Peanuts on drinks cupboard
Off Stage	Letters, breakfast tray, newspaper (Rahmu)
	Breakfast tray & hat in hatbox (Houseboy)

Act TWO, Scene 1

On stage	Gun set beside piano (Auntie)
	Smelling salts (Vana)
	Workbasket, crochet hook & wool
	Hatbox
Off stage	Bottle of Tizer (Rahmu)
	Cardboard box containing large black spider (Jeremy)
	Copy of Will (Rahmu)

Act TWO, Scene 2

On stage   Hatbox

Ornament on desk

Off stage   Scarf & handkerchief (Beatrice)

Umbrella (Rahmu)

Act TWO, Scene 3

On stage   Record

Jug of water on drinks cupboard

Paper on desk

Off stage   Assortment of curry dishes, cutlery, etc. on
trolley (Rahmu)

Handbag (Vana)

Scarf (Rahmu)

VERANDAH BACKING

DOOR

SHRUBBERY BACKING

DRINKS CUPBOARD

STOOL

VERANDAH

SETTEE

STEPS (OPTIONAL)

ARMCHAIR

TABLE

DOUBLE DOORS

GARDEN BACKING

GUN CABINET

DESK

STAGE PLAN

MOVE OVER MRS MARKHAM

RAY COONEY & JOHN CHAPMAN

Move Over Mrs Markham exposes the intricacies and complications which ensue when different sets of hopeful lovers all converge upon the bedroom of the Markhams' supposedly empty flat. The complications and deceptions which follow assure a hectic and hilarious evening.

For further details contact Chappell Plays Ltd, 129 Park Street, London W1Y 3FA.

NOT NOW DARLING
RAY COONEY & JOHN CHAPMAN

Not Now Darling is set in an elegant West End fur salon where the hilarious permutations and entanglements reach a point of hysteria before everyone gets their just desserts. A truly uproarious farce about the consequences of attempted infidelity.

For further details contact Chappell Plays Ltd, 129 Park Street, London W1Y 3FA.